༄༅། །ཕྱག་རྒྱ་ཆེན་པོའི་ཁྲིད་ཡིག་ཆེན་མོ་
གཉུག་མའི་དེ་ཉིད་གསལ་བ་ཞེས་བྱ་བ་བཞུགས་སོ།།

Clarifying the Natural State

Rangjung Yeshe Books ♦ www.rangjung.com

PADMASAMBHAVA ♦ *Treasures from Juniper Ridge* ♦ *Advice from the Lotus-Born* ♦ *Dakini Teachings*

PADMASAMBHAVA AND JAMGÖN KONGTRÜL ♦ *The Light of Wisdom, Vol. 1, Vol. 2, Vol. 3, Vol. 4, & Vol. 5*

PADMASAMBHAVA, CHOKGYUR LINGPA, TULKU URGYEN RINPOCHE, ORGYEN TOPGYAL RINPOCHE, AND LAMA PUTSI PEMA TASHI ♦ *Dispeller of Obstacles*

YESHE TSOGYAL ♦ *The Lotus-Born*

DAKPO TASHI NAMGYAL ♦ *Clarifying the Natural State*

TSELE NATSOK RANGDRÖL ♦ *Mirror of Mindfulness* ♦ *Empowerment* ♦ *Heart Lamp*

CHOKGYUR LINGPA ♦ *Ocean of Amrita* ♦ *The Great Gate* ♦ *Skillful Grace* ♦ *Great Accomplishment*

TRAKTUNG DUDJOM LINGPA ♦ *A Clear Mirror*

JAMGÖN MIPHAM RINPOCHE ♦ *Gateway to Knowledge, Vol. 1, Vol. 2, Vol. 3, & Vol. 4*

TULKU URGYEN RINPOCHE ♦ *Blazing Splendor* ♦ *Rainbow Painting* ♦ *As It Is, Vol. 1 & Vol. 2* ♦ *Vajra Speech* ♦ *Repeating the Words of the Buddha*

ADEU RINPOCHE ♦ *Freedom in Bondage*

KHENCHEN THRANGU RINPOCHE ♦ *King of Samadhi* ♦ *Crystal Clear*

CHÖKYI NYIMA RINPOCHE ♦ *Present Fresh Wakefulness*

TULKU THONDUP ♦ *Enlightened Living*

ORGYEN TOBGYAL RINPOCHE ♦ *Life & Teachings of Chokgyur Lingpa*

DZIGAR KONGTRÜL RINPOCHE ♦ *Uncommon Happiness*

TSOKNYI RINPOCHE ♦ *Fearless Simplicity* ♦ *Carefree Dignity*

DZOGCHEN TRILOGY COMPILED BY MARCIA BINDER SCHMIDT ♦ *Dzogchen Primer* ♦ *Dzogchen Essentials* ♦ *Quintessential Dzogchen*

ERIK PEMA KUNSANG ♦ *Wellsprings of the Great Perfection* ♦ *A Tibetan Buddhist Companion* ♦ *The Rangjung Yeshe Tibetan-English Dictionary of Buddhist Culture & Perfect Clarity*

MARCIA DECHEN WANGMO ♦ *Confessions of a Gypsy Yogini* ♦ *Precious Songs of Awakening compilation*

CHOKGYUR LINGPA, JAMGÖN KONGTRÜL, JAMYANG KHYENTSE WANGPO, ADEU RINPOCHE, AND ORGYEN TOPGYAL RINPOCHE ♦ *The Tara Compendium Feminine Principles Discovered*

Clarifying the Natural State

A Principal Guidance Manual for Mahamudra

by

Dakpo Tashi Namgyal

Foreword by
KHENCHEN THRANGU RINPOCHE

Translated from the Tibetan by
ERIK PEMA KUNSANG

Edited by
MICHAEL TWEED

RANGJUNG YESHE • *Boudhanath, Hong Kong & Esby* • 2001

Rangjung Yeshe Publications
125 Robinson Road, flat 6a
Hong Kong

Address letters to:
Rangjung Yeshe Publications
P.O. Box 1200
Kathmandu, Nepal

www.rangjung.com
office@rangjung.com

First edition 2001

Printed in the United States of America
on recycled acid-free paper
3 5 7 9 8 6 4

Distributed to the book trade by Publishers Group West

Publication Data:

ISBN 978-962-7341-45-1 (pbk.)

Author: Dakpo Tashi Namgyal
(*dvags po bkra shis rnam rgyal*), (1512–1587).
Foreword by Khenchen Thrangu Rinpoche (b. 1933).
Translated from the Tibetan by Erik Pema Kunsang
(Erik Hein Schmidt). Edited by Michael Tweed.
First Ed.
Title: Clarifying the Natural State;
A Principal Guidance Manual for Mahamudra
Tibetan Title: *phyag rgya chen po'i khrid yig chen mo gnyug ma'i de nyid gsal ba.*

1. Vajrayana/Mahamudra—tradition of pith instructions.
2. Buddhism — Tibet.
I Title

Contents

Introduction 9

Opening Verses 13

PART ONE
PRELIMINARY STEPS OF GUIDANCE

General Preliminaries 15

Specific Preliminaries 15

PART TWO
THE MAIN PART OF THE MEDITATION STAGES

Steps of Guidance 17

Guidance Through Shamatha 17

Shamatha with Attributes 17

Supported Shamatha 17

Unsupported Shamatha 19

Shamatha with Breathing Practice 19

Shamatha without Breathing Practice 21

Shamatha without Attributes 23

Tightening 23

Loosening 24

Guiding by Means of Vipashyana 26

Establishing the Identity of Mind and the Various Perceptions 27

Establishing the Identity of Mind — the Basis 27
Establishing the Identity of Thoughts and Perceptions — the Expression 29

Clearing Up Uncertainties About Basis and Expression 31
Resolving That Thoughts Are Mind 32
Resolving That Perceptions Are Mind 34
Investigating the Calm and the Moving mind 36
Resolving That All Experience Is Nonarising 37

Steps of Pointing-Out Instruction 40
The Actual Pointing Out of the Innate 40
Pointing Out Innate Mind-Essence 40
Pointing Out Innate Thinking 43
Pointing Out Innate Perception 45
Eradicating Faults and Identifying the Meditation Practice 47
Describing Mistakes and Faulty Meditation 47
Explaining Flawless Meditation Practice 50

PART THREE
SUBSEQUENT WAYS TO CONTINUE THE TRAINING

General Reasons for Meditation Training 53

Special Training without Separating Meditation and Postmeditation 55

Cutting through Hindrances, Sidetracks and Straying 59

Sidetracks 61

Enhancing by Transcending into Nonarising 64
The Time for Transcending 64

Investigating Thoughts and Perceptions 65
Investigating the Meditation and the Meditating Mind 66
The Actual Transcending into Nonarising Openness 67
Mingling Meditation and Postmeditation, Day and Night 69
Developing Strength by Utilizing the Conducts 70
The Time for Utilizing and the Conducts 70
Utilizing Thoughts 72
Utilizing Emotions 73
Utilizing Gods and Demons 73
Utilizing Suffering 74
Utilizing Sickness 74
Utilizing the Process of Dying 75
How Realization Arises and the Enhancement Practices 76
The Various Ways Realization Arises 77
One-Pointedness and Its Enhancement 78
Simplicity and Its Enhancement 84
One Taste and Its Enhancement 89
Nonmeditation and Its Enhancement 95

PART FOUR
THE WAY TO TRAVERSE THE PATHS AND BHUMIS THROUGH MEDITATION TRAINING 101
Concluding Verses 103
Colophon 104

Translator's Colophon 105
Endnotes 106

THE VERY VENERABLE

THRANGU RINPOCHE

༄༅། །དེང་གི་དུས་དད་པས་རྗེས་འབྲང་ཙམ་མ་ཡིན་པར། དབང་རྟོན་ཆོས་ཀྱི་རྗེས་སུ་འབྲང་བའི་བློ་ནས་ཕྱི་ནང་གི་ཤེས་ཡོན་ཅན་མང་པོ་ཞིག་གིས་དམ་པའི་ཆོས་ཀྱི་ཉམས་ལེན་ལ་འབད་བརྩོན་གནང་བཞིན་པའི་སྐབས། ཟབ་དོན་མཐར་ཐུག་པ་ཕྱག་རྫོགས་ཀྱི་མན་ངག་དང་ལྡན་པ་ཞིག་དགོས་ལ། དེ་ལས་ཀྱང་དམ་ཆོས་ཕྱག་རྒྱ་ཆེན་པོ་ནི་གདམས་ངག་ཟབ་ལ་ཉམས་སུ་ལེན་བདེ་བ། རྒྱ་གར་འཕགས་པའི་ཡུལ་གྱི་གྲུབ་ཐོབ་ཆེན་པོ་བརྒྱད་དང་། བརྒྱད་ཅུ་ཐོན་པ་རྣམས་ཀྱི་དགོངས་བཅུད་མ་ཉམས་པ་ད་ལྟ་བོད་ཀྱི་མཁས་གྲུབ་ཆེན་པོ་རྣམས་ཀྱིས་འཆད་ཉན་དང་ཉམས་བཞེས་ཀྱི་རྒྱུན་མ་ཉམས་པར་ཞུགས་པ་ཁག་ཕྱི་རྒྱལ་གྱི་སྐད་ཡིག་ཐོག་ཕབ་བསྒྱུར་གནང་རྒྱུ་ཤིན་ཏུ་གལ་ཆེ་ཞིང་། ལྷག་པར་དྭགས་པོ་བཀྲ་ཤིས་རྣམ་རྒྱལ་གྱི་གསུང་རྣམས་ནི། གཞན་དང་མི་འདྲ་བའི་སྒོམ་ཐོག་ནས་བྱུང་བའི་མན་ངག་མང་པོས་བརྒྱན་པ་ཡིན་པའི་ཕྱིར་ན། ཉམས་ལེན་གནང་བ་པོ་རྣམས་ཀྱི་གེགས་སེལ་དང་། བོག་འདོན་སོགས་གང་ལ་ཡང་ཤིན་ཏུ་ཕན་པ་ཆེ་བའི་མན་ངག་ཡིན་པར་བརྟེན། ཕྱག་རྒྱ་ཆེན་པོའི་སྒོམ་རིམ་ཟླ་བའི་འོད་ཟེར་དང་། གཉུག་མའི་དེ་ཉིད་གསལ་བ་གཉིས་ནི་ཁྱད་པར་དུ་འཕགས་ཤིང་། དེ་གཉིས་ལས་ཀྱང་ཕྱི་མ་འདི་ནི་ཉམས་ལེན་ཁོ་ན་གཙོ་བོར་གནང་བས་མེད་དུ་མི་རུང་བ་ཞིག་ཡིན་པ་དང་། མ་ཟད་བསྒྱུར་བ་པོ་ཡང་སྐད་ཡིག་རྒྱང་པ་ལ་མཁས་པ་ཙམ་མ་ཡིན་པར། སྒོམ་གྱི་ཉམས་མྱོང་ཚུང་ཟད་ཡོད་པ་གལ་ཆེ་བས། ལོ་ཙཱ་བ་ཨེར་རིག་པདྨ་ཀུན་བཟང་ནི། སྤྲུལ་སྐུ་ཨོ་རྒྱན་རིན་པོ་ཆེ་ཡུན་རིང་དུ་བསྟེན་ཞིང་གསུང་བསྒྱུར་ཞུས་པས་སྒོམ་གྱི་ཉམས་མྱོང་ཡོད་པར་བརྟེན། ཁོང་གིས་དབྱིན་སྐད་དུ་ཕབ་བསྒྱུར་གྲུབ་པ་ལ་སྙིང་ཐག་པ་ནས་ཐུགས་རྗེ་ཆེ་ཞུ། །ཞེས་ཁྲ་འགུ་སྤྲུལ་མིང་པས། ༢༠༠༧ ཕྱི་ཟླ་ ༢ ཚེས་ ༨ ལ།།

THRANGU TASHI CHOELING, P.O. BOX 1287, BOUDDHA, KATHMANDU, NEPAL. PHONE: 470028

Introduction

These days many people follow the Dharma astutely and not merely out of faith. Knowledgeable in many topics, they exert themselves in applying the sublime teachings. So, it is important that the profound and ultimate instructions of Mahamudra and Dzogchen are made available. These should include the sublime teachings of Mahamudra, the profound instructions that are simple to practice that are the unimpaired essence of realization of the eight great masters and eighty mahasiddhas from the noble land of India. As these instructions have been kept alive, through an unbroken stream of teaching and practice, by the learned and accomplished masters of Tibet, I find it of vital importance to have some of them translated into foreign languages.

In particular, the words of Dakpo Tashi Namgyal are unique in that they are adorned with plenty of pithy advice out of his personal experience. Therefore, practitioners are greatly benefited by his instructions on how to remove hindrances and progress further. His methods for practicing Mahamudra, found in such books as *Moonbeams* and *Clarifying the Natural State,* are preeminent. Of these, this book is indispensable as it focuses exclusively on practice.

Moreover, it is vital for the translator of such works to be not only skilled in language, but also possess some degree of meditation experience. The lotsawa Erik Pema Kunsang was the attendant of and translated for Tulku Urgyen Rinpoche for many years and is experienced in meditation, I am therefore sincerely grateful that he has completed this English translation.

Signed by the bearer of the name Thrangu Tulku,
on February 4th 2001.

"Mahamudra"

calligraphy, Thrangu Rinpoche

༄༅། ཕྱག་རྒྱ་ཆེན་པོའི་ཁྲིད་ཡིག་ཆེན་མོ་ གཉུག་མའི་དེ་ཉིད་གསལ་བ་ཞེས་བྱ་བ་བཞུགས་སོ།།

ངེས་དོན་ཕྱག་རྒྱ་ཆེན་པོའི་སྒོམ་ཁྲིད་ཀྱི་རིམ་པ་གཉུག་མའི་དེ་ཉིད་གསལ་བ་ཞེས་བྱ་བ།

བླ་མ་དང་དཔལ་རྡོ་རྗེ་འཆང་ལ་གུས་པས་ཕྱག་འཚལ་ལོ།།

ཆོས་དབྱིངས་སྟོང་ཉིད་སྤྲོས་བྲལ་རང་བཞིན་ལས།།
སྣང་སྲིད་སྒྱུ་མའི་བཀོད་པ་ཟབ་གསལ་ཅན།།
གདོད་ནས་ལྷུན་གྲུབ་བདེ་སྟོང་ཟུང་འཇུག་བདག།
ཀུན་ཁྱབ་རྣལ་མའི་སེམས་ལ་གུས་པས་འདུད།།

ལམ་གཞན་དག་གིས་ཡུན་རིང་རྟོགས་དཀའ་བའི།།
ངེས་གསང་ཁྱབ་བདག་སེམས་ཀྱི་མངོན་རྟོགས་གང་།།
ཚེགས་མེད་མཛུབ་ཚུགས་ལྟ་བུར་སྟོན་མཛད་པ།།
སྒམ་པོ་པར་གྲགས་སྒྲུབ་བརྒྱུད་བཅས་ལ་འདུད།།

The Steps for Guidance in the Mahamudra of Definitive Meaning Entitled Clarifying the Natural State

Respectful homage to glorious Vajradhara.

Out of the unconstructed nature, the emptiness of
dharmadhatu,
Appear the magical sceneries of the worlds and beings,
profound and brilliant.
To their indivisible identity of empty bliss, spontaneously
present from the beginning,
To the all-pervasive original mind, I respectfully bow
down.

The true realization of mind, the all-pervasive identity of
the definitive secret,
Is difficult to realize through other long-lasting paths;
Yet, you reveal it effortlessly, like pointing to it
with your finger —
To the illustrious Gampopa and the masters of the
Practice Lineage, I bow down.

དེ་ཡི་ལམ་ལ་ཕྱག་རྒྱ་ཆེན་པོ་ཞེས།།

ཉི་ཟླ་ལྟར་གྲགས་གངས་ཅན་གསལ་བྱས་མོད།།

འོན་ཀྱང་ཉམས་མྱོང་མན་ངག་གིས་བརྒྱན་ཏེ།།

རྟོག་གེ་སྤྱངས་ནས་སླར་ཡང་གསལ་བརྗོད་བྱ།།

དེ་ལ་འདིར་འཁོར་བའི་སྡུག་བསྔལ་མཐའ་དག་གིས་ཡིད་རབ་ཏུ་སྐྱོ་ནས་མྱུར་དུ་སངས་རྒྱས་སྒྲུབ་པའི་ངེས་འབྱུང་དྲག་པོ་དང་ལྡན་ཞིང་། རྟོགས་ལྡན་གྱི་བླ་མ་དང་བྱིན་རླབས་ཀྱི་ལམ་ལ་དད་ཅིང་ཡིད་ཆེས་པའི་སྐལ་པ་ཅན་དག་བདེ་བླག་ཉིད་དུ་གནས་ལུགས་ཀྱི་དོན་ལ་འགོད་པར་བྱ་བ་ངེས་དོན་ཕྱག་རྒྱ་ཆེན་པོའི་ཁྲིད་ཀྱི་རིམ་པ་ལ་བཞི།

ཁྲིད་རིམ་གྱི་སྔོན་འགྲོ།

སྒོམ་རིམ་གྱི་དངོས་གཞི།

རྗེས་ཉམས་ལེན་སྐྱོང་ཚུལ།

སྒོམ་སྤྱངས་པས་ས་ལམ་བགྲོད་ཚུལ་ལོ།།

His practice tradition known as Mahamudra,
Celebrated like the sun and the moon, has illuminated
this Land of Snow.
Even so, here I shall set intellectual arguments aside and
clarify it once more,
Adorned with the pith instructions of personal experience.

This manual for guidance in the Mahamudra of the definitive meaning is meant for worthy people who are utterly weary of all of samsara's miseries, who possess the intense renunciation of wishing to quickly attain enlightenment, and who have trust and confidence in the realized masters and the path of blessings. To establish them straightforwardly in the meaning of the natural state, there are four parts:

Preliminary steps of guidance
The main part of the meditation stages
Subsequent ways to continue the training
The way to traverse the paths and bhumis through meditation training

དང་པོ་ལ་གཉིས།

ཐུན་མོང་གི་སྨོན་འགྲོ་དང་།

ཐུན་མོང་མ་ཡིན་པའི་སྨོན་འགྲོའོ།།

དང་པོ་ནི། ཐུར་དུ་བཤད་པ་ལྟར་དལ་འབྱོར་རྙེད་དཀའ་བ་དང་མི་རྟག་པ་བསམ་པ་སོགས་སྐྱེས་བུ་གསུམ་གྱི་ལམ་རིམ་ཅི་རིགས་པ་བསྒོམ་དུ་བཅུག་ལ་ངེས་འབྱུང་གི་བློ་བརྟན་པོ་བསྐྱེད་པ་གལ་ཆེ་སྟེ།

འདིར་ནན་ཏན་མ་བྱས་པར་སླ་ཆོས་སུ་བྱས་ན། ལན་རེ་ཙམ་གྱིས་གོ་ཡུལ་དུ་ལུས་ནས་སྐྱབས་པ་བརྟོན་པ་མི་སྐྱེ་ཞིང་ཆོས་བརྒྱུད་ཀྱི་དབང་དུ་འགྲོ་བ་ཡིན་ནོ།།

གཉིས་པ་ནི། གསང་སྔགས་བླ་མེད་ཀྱི་དཀྱིལ་འཁོར་དུ་སྨིན་བྱེད་ཀྱི་དབང་བསྐུར་རྒྱས་པར་བྱ་བའམ་བྱིན་རླབས་བརྡའི་དབང་ལ་སོགས་པས་སྨིན་པར་བྱས་ལ།

Part One
Preliminary Steps of Guidance

This has two steps:
General preliminaries
Specific preliminaries

General Preliminaries

As explained elsewhere, practitioners should thoroughly train in the gradual stages of the path for the three types of individual.[1] This includes the reflections on the difficult-to-acquire freedoms and riches, impermanence and so forth. In this way, it is essential to develop a firm attitude of renunciation.

If students do not do so keenly, but instead regard these topics as trivial, they will, after hearing the four mind-changings a few times, leave them behind as mere information. Having done so, they will not exert themselves in practice and become caught up in the eight worldly concerns.

Specific Preliminaries

Second, practitioners should be brought to maturation either by receiving the ripening empowerment within the Anuttara mandalas of the Secret Mantra or through the symbolic empowerment of blessings.

དེ་ནས་ཟུར་དུ་བཤད་པ་ལྟར།

ལེ་ལོ་བཟློག་ཕྱིར་མི་རྟག་པ་བསམ་པ།

བར་ཆད་སེལ་ཕྱིར་སྐྱབས་འགྲོ་སེམས་བསྐྱེད།

ཚོགས་བསགས་ཕྱིར་མཎྜལ་དབུལ་བ།

སྒྲིབ་པ་སྦྱང་ཕྱིར་རྡོར་སེམས་ཀྱི་སྒོམ་བཟླས།

བྱིན་རླབས་འཇུག་ཕྱིར་བླ་མའི་རྣལ་འབྱོར་སྒོམ་པ་རྣམས་རིམ་པས་ཁྲིད་དེ།

དེ་དག་རེ་རེ་ལ་ཞག་ལྔའམ་བདུན་ལ་སོགས་པ་ཅི་རིགས་པར་འབད་དུ་བཙུག་ཅིང་རྣལ་འབྱོར་རེའི་མཇུག་ཏུ་སེམས་ལྟོད་དེ་བ་འཐོལ་ལེ་བ་ལ་ཅི་གནས་འཇོག་ཏུ་བཙུག་ལ་ཉམས་ཚོད་བྱའོ།།

Following that, as explained elsewhere, to ward off laziness reflect on impermanence; to dispel obstacles take refuge and form the bodhisattva resolve; to gather the accumulations offer mandalas; to purify obscurations do the meditation and recitation of Vajrasattva; and to receive blessings train in guru yoga. Receive guidance in all of these points one after another and exert yourself in each of them for a suitable number of days, such as five or seven. At the end of each of these practices, gain some experience by relaxing your mind and remaining free and easy for as long as you can.

གཉིས་པ་སྒོམ་རིམ་གྱི་དངོས་གཞི་ལ་གཉིས།

ཁྲིད་པའི་རིམ་པ་དང་།

ངོ་སྤྲོད་པའི་རིམ་པའོ།།

དང་པོ་ལ་གཉིས།

ཞི་གནས་ཀྱི་སྒོ་ནས་ཁྲིད་པ་དང་།

ལྷག་མཐོང་གི་སྒོ་ནས་ཁྲིད་པའོ།།

དང་པོ་ལ་གཉིས།

མཚན་བཅས་དང་།

མཚན་མེད་དོ།།

དང་པོ་ལ་གཉིས།

རྟེན་ཅན་དང་། རྟེན་མེད་དོ།།

དང་པོ་ནི། ཐུན་བཞི་ལ་སོགས་པར་སྔོན་འགྲོའི་རྣལ་འབྱོར་རྣམས་སྔར་བས་ཐུན་ཆུང་བ་མ་ཆགས་ཙམ་རེ་བྱ་ཞིང་།

བླ་མའི་རྣལ་འབྱོར་གྱི་སྐབས་སུ་ཁྱད་པར་ཏིང་ངེ་འཛིན་སྐྱེ་བར་གསོལ་བ་དྲག་ཏུ་བཏབ།

Part Two
The Main Part of the Meditation Stages

This has two parts:
Steps of guidance
Steps of pointing-out instruction

Steps of Guidance

This has two points:
Guidance through shamatha
Guidance through vipashyana

Guidance Through Shamatha

This has two steps:
Shamatha with attributes
Shamatha without attributes

Shamatha with Attributes

This has two parts:
Supported shamatha
Unsupported shamatha

Supported Shamatha

In your four sessions continue the preliminary practices, not as extensively as before, but without ever missing a day. At the time of guru yoga, make particularly deep-felt supplications that samadhi may take birth.

དེ་ནས་རྐང་པ་རྡོ་རྗེ་སྐྱིལ་ཀྲུང་ངམ་མ་ནུས་ན་སེམས་དཔའི་སྐྱིལ་ཀྲུང་བྱ། ལག་པ་མཉམ་བཞག་གི་ཕྱག་རྒྱ་ལྟེ་འོག་སོར་བཞིའི་ཐད་དུ་བསྣོམ། སྒལ་པ་བསྲང་ཞིང་ལུས་ཀུན་བསྒྲིམ། དཔུང་པ་དང་གྲུ་མོ་མ་གཡུག་པར་བརྒྱང་། མགྲིན་པར་ཙུང་ཟད་བཀུག །ལྕེ་རྩེ་ཡ་རྐན་ལ་གཏད་དེ་སོ་ལ་བར་བག་ཙམ་ཡོད་པ་བྱས་ལ་མཆུ་བཙུམ། མིག་སྣ་རྩེའི་ཐད་ཀར་ཞི་བའི་ལྟ་སྟངས་བྱ་བ་སྟེ་ལུས་རྣམས་སྣང་གི་ཆོས་བདུན་དང་ལྡན་པར་འདུག་གོ།།

སྤྱིར་བསམ་གཏན་མཐའ་དག་ལ་ལུས་ཀྱི་འཁྲུལ་འཁོར་གནད་ཆེ་ཞིང་། ཁྱད་པར་སེམས་གནས་པ་ལ་ལུས་གནད་ཤིན་ཏུ་གལ་ཆེ་བས་ནན་ཏན་ཆེར་བྱེད་དུ་བཙུག་ན་འགའ་ཞིག་ལ་འདིར་རང་གིས་གནས་ཆ་སྙེད་པ་འོང་ཞིང་། ལུས་གནད་ཉིན་ཞག་འགའ་སྐྱོང་བ་བྱུང་ཡང་ལེགས་སོ།།

དེ་ནས་ཉིན་མོ་ལྟ་སྟངས་ཀྱི་ཐད་ཀར་རྡེའུ་འམ་ཤིང་བུ་སོགས་ཀྱི་རྟེན་དཀར་མདངས་ཅན་མིན་པ་ཞིག་བཞག་སྟེ། དེ་ལ་སེམས་ལྷོད་ཀྱིས་གཏད་པ་ཙམ་བྱ་ཞིང་དེ་ཉིད་ལ་ཙིར་འཛིན་དང་བརྟག་དཔྱད་ཀྱང་མི་བྱ། སེམས་གཞན་དུ་ནམ་ཡང་མ་འཕྲོས་མ་ཡེངས་ཙམ་བྱས་ལ་གནས་སུ་འཇུག་པ་དང་། ཡང་ཉི་གྲིབ་ཀྱི་མཚམས་སུ་ཟླ་ས་ཆུང་ངུ་ཞིག་ལ་གོང་ལྟར་སེམས་གཟུང་བ་རྣམས་བྱ།

མཚན་མོ་རང་གི་སྨིན་མཚམས་སུ་ཐིག་ལེ་དཀར་པོ་སྲན་མ་ཙམ་ལ་སེམས་འཛིན་པ་དང་། རེས་རང་གི་འོག་ཏུ་ཐིག་ལེ་ནག་པོ་སྲན་མ་ཙམ་ལ་སེམས་གཟུང་བ་གོང་བཞིན་བྱ།

After that, place your legs in the vajra posture, or if you cannot, then in the *sattva* posture. Join your hands four fingers below the navel in the gesture of equanimity. Align your backbone and straighten your entire body; extend your shoulders and elbows until they too are straight. Slightly tilt your neck.[2] Connect the tip of your tongue to the palate and close your lips with a slight space between the teeth. Your eyes should assume a peaceful gaze directed at the level of your nose tip. In this way, sit in the sevenfold posture of Vairochana.

Generally speaking, body posture is important in all meditation practice. Specifically, the physical key points are essential for quieting the mind. This is why, when it is emphasized, some people find calm simply through this posture and also why it would be excellent to train for several days in simply keeping the body posture.

Then, during the daytime, place a support, such as a pebble or a stick that isn't too bright, directly in line with your gaze. In a relaxed way, direct your attention at it without fixating on it or examining it. Allow your attention to remain on the object of support simply to avoid wandering off or being distracted.

Next, keep the attention, as above, on a small object that has been placed on the borderline between shade and sunlight. At night, focus the attention on a pea-sized white sphere between the eyebrows. At times, direct the mind, as before, on a pea-sized black sphere below you.

A certain type of person will find it hard to gain calmness and will grow tired of these ways of focusing the

གནས་ཆ་སྙིང་དཀའ་བའི་རིགས་སེམས་འཛིན་པ་དེ་དག་གིས་དུབ་པ་ལ། མདུན་གྱི་ནམ་མཁར་དེ་བཞིན་གཤེགས་པའི་སྐུ་ཆེན་གང་བ་བསྒོམས་པའི་སྐུའི་ཆ་ལ་སེམས་གཟུང་བ་སོགས་སྣ་ཚོགས་པ་བྱ་བར་བཤད་ཀྱང་ཕལ་ཆེར་ལ་འདི་ཙམ་གྱིས་ཆོག་གོ།

གནས་ཆ་སྙིང་ན་གནས་རང་བཞིན་གྱི་ངང་ལས་ཤིགས་བཤིགས་ལ་ཙུང་ཟད་ཙམ་ངལ་གསོ། ཐུན་ཆུང་ལ་གྲངས་མང་དུ་བྱ།

ཐུན་བར་དུ་ལྟད་མོ་ལྟ་བ་དང་སྤྱོད་ལམ་དྲག་པོ་དང་སྨྲ་བ་མང་པོ་རྣམས་སྤང་ཞིང་ལུས་སེམས་དལ་དུ་བཏུག་གོ།།

གཉིས་པ་རྟེན་མེད་ལ་གཉིས། རླུང་ཅན་དང་། རླུང་མེད་དོ།།

དང་པོ་ནི། ཐོག་མར་རླུང་བགྲང་བ་ལ་བརྟེན་ནས་སེམས་གཟུང་བ་ནི། རླུང་ཕྱིར་འགྲོ་བ་དང་ནང་དུ་འོང་བ་གཉིས་དྲན་ཙམ་བྱ་ཞིང་གཞན་དུ་སེམས་མ་ཡེངས་པར་བྱས་ཏེ། རླུང་ཁུག་པ་དང་པོར་གསུམ་དེ་ནས་བདུན་སོགས་ཅི་རིགས་ལ་སེམས་བཟུང་ཞིང་། སེམས་འཚུབས་ན་སྐབས་སུ་ཙུང་ཟད་རེ་ངལ་གསོས་ལ་སྤྱང་དུ་བཏུག་སྟེ་ཉམས་བལྟ།

དེ་ནས་རླུང་དགང་བ་ལ་བརྟེན་ནས་སེམས་གཟུང་བ་ནི། རླུང་རེ་གསུམ་མམ་དགུ་བུས་ལ་སྣ་གཉིས་ནས་དལ་བུས་རྔུབ་ཏེ་མཆིལ་མ་ཞིག་མེད་པ་དང་བཅས་པས་ཧ་ཅང་མནན་དྲག་པོ་མིན་པར་གསུས་པར་ཆིལ་གྱིས་མནན།

attention. They should imagine the bodily form of the Tathagata, the size of one inch, right in the sky before them. Although a variety of other such ways of concentrating the attention are taught, for most people this will suffice.

Once you have achieved a natural sense of calm, interrupt the practice and take a short break. Do short sessions but repeated many times.

In between sessions avoid entertainment, strenuous activities and much talk. Keep both body and mind quiet.

Unsupported Shamatha

This has two parts:
With breathing practice
Without breathing practice

Shamatha with Breathing Practice

First, to focus the attention by counting the breath, remain aware of the inhalation and exhalation enough to avoid drifting off toward other things. Begin by focusing on three rounds of breathing, then on seven and so forth — whatever is appropriate. If your attention gets restless, take a little rest from time to time and then continue the training so as to gain some experience.

Next, to center the attention by holding the breath, expel the stale air three or nine times. Gently inhale through the two nostrils. Together with swallowing the saliva, press down the stomach with some force, but not too hard. For as long as you can, simply keep from wandering off; do not become absent-minded. When you are no longer able

དེ་ཅི་ཐུབ་ཀྱི་བར་སེམས་མ་འཕྲོས་ཙམ་ཏད་དེ་སེམས་མི་འདུག། མི་ཐུབ་ན་སྣ་ནས་དལ་བུས་བཏང་ཞིང་ཕྱིར་འགྲོ་བ་དང་ནང་དུ་འོང་བའི་ཚེ་སྔར་བཞིན་འགྲོ་འོང་དྲན་སེམས་ཙམ་ལས་སེམས་གཞན་དུ་མ་འཕྲོས་པ་བྱ།

ངལ་ན་རླུང་སྣ་བུག་ནས་ཅི་བདེར་འགྲོ་འོང་བྱེད་དུ་བཅུག་ཅིང་སེམས་གཞན་དུ་མ་ཡེངས་པར་ལྷོད་དེ་སང་ངེ་བར་དྲན་པས་ཟིན་ཙམ་བྱ།

ཅུང་ཟད་རེ་ངལ་གསོ་ཞིང་སླར་ཡང་དེ་ལྟར་སྦྱང་དུ་བཅུག་ལ་ཉམས་བལྟ། དེ་ལྟར་བྱས་པས་སེམས་རྒོད་དུ་སོང་ན་ཧ་ཅང་བསྒྲིམས་པའི་སྐྱོན་ཡིན་པས་ཁོང་གློད།

སེམས་པ་ན་སུན་མང་ཞིང་ཤིན་ཏུ་འཚུབ་ན་དུབ་པ་ཡིན་པས་ཞག་རེ་ཙམ་ཁམས་གསེང་བྱ། མགོ་འཁོར་བ་དང་སེམས་ཡེར་ན་རླུང་གིས་བསྐྱོད་པས་བཟའ་བཏུང་བཅུད་ཆེ་བ་ལ་བསྟེན་ཞིང་བསྐུ་མཉེ་བྱེད་དུ་བཅུག།

འདི་ཡན་ཆད་ལ་སེམས་མ་ཟིན་པ་ཟིན་པར་བྱེད་པ་ཞེས་བྱ་སྟེ་སེམས་ཀྱི་གནས་ཆ་རྙེད་པ་བྱ་དགོས་སོ།།

གལ་ཏེ་འདི་དག་གི་ཚེ་སེམས་འགྱུ་བ་མང་དུ་སོང་བ་ལྟར་གྱུར་ནས་གནས་ཆ་ཆུང་ན། སྔར་རྣམ་རྟོག་ལུ་གུ་རྒྱུད་དུ་འཕྲོས་པ་ཐམས་ཅད་མ་རིག་པ་ལ་འདིར་རྣམ་རྟོག་གཅིག་སྐྱེས་གཉིས་སྐྱེས་རིག་པས་འཕྲིག་ཚུད་ཅིང་གནས་ཆ་ཅུང་ཟད་རྙེད་པ་ཡིན་པས་སྐྱོན་དུ་མི་གཟུང་ཞིང་།

to hold, exhale gently through the nose. While exhaling and inhaling as before, keep attentive of the breathing at least enough so as not to wander off to other things.

When tired, inhale and exhale freely through the nose. Keep your attention relaxed and clear, with enough mindfulness so as not to become distracted by anything else. Every once in a while take a rest. Continue training in this way until you gain some experience.

If your attention becomes more agitated while doing this, it is due to being too focused, so relax from within.

If you become repeatedly bored and very restless, it is due to being tired out, so refresh yourself for a couple of days.

If you get dizzy and light-headed, it is due to the influence of *wind*, so take more nutritious food and drink, and do massage.[3]

The steps up to this point are known as *capturing the uncaught mind*. They are necessary to achieve mental calm.

If, during these steps, you feel that mental movements have increased and you are less calm, this is because of formerly not noticing all the thought-trains being projected. Now, you do notice one thought arising after the other. You have become aware and gained some calm, so do not regard this as a shortcoming. Do not direct the thought and do not pursue it. Rather, rest loosely and continue to apply yourself. By doing so you will experience calm.

རྟོག་པའི་སྣ་མི་བསྐྱིལ་རྗེས་མི་འབྲང་བར་ལྷོད་དེ་བཞག་པ་ལ་འབད་དུ་བཙུག་པས་གནས་པ་འཆར་རོ།།

གལ་ཏེ་སེམས་འཕྲོས་པ་དང་གནས་པའི་དབྱིབས་གང་ཡང་མ་རིག་པར་ཁྲུ་འཕྲིག་མ་བྱུང་ན། ཕཊ་ཅེས་པའི་སྒྲ་དྲག་པོའི་རྗེས་སམ་འབོད་སྐད་དྲག་པོ་ལྟ་བུའི་དུས་རྟོག་པ་སྔ་མ་རྒྱུན་ཆད་ཕྱི་མ་མ་སྐྱེས་པའི་བར་གྱི་སེམས་ལྟ་བུ་རྟོག་མེད་ཀྱི་གནས་ཆ་ཡིན་པ་དང་།

དེ་ནས་འདི་བྱ་འདི་བྱེད་ཀྱི་བློ་སྐྱེས་པ་སོགས་རྣམ་རྟོག་འཕྲོས་པ་ཡིན་པའི་བརྡ་དོན་སྤྲོད་ལ། རེས་བསྒྲིམ་རེས་གློད་པ་སོགས་ཐབས་སྣ་ཚོགས་པའི་སྒོ་ནས་ཁྲིད་མཁས་བྱས་ལ་འཕྲིག་ཚུད་དུ་བཙུག་སྟེ་ནན་གྱིས་སྦྱངས་པས་གནས་ཆ་རྙེད་པར་འགྱུར་རོ།།

གཉིས་པ་རླུང་མེད་ནི། དེ་ལྟར་སེམས་ཀྱི་གནས་ཆ་ཅི་རིགས་རྙེད་ནས། ལུས་གནད་སྔར་ལྟར་བྱས་ལ་ཕྱིའི་གཟུགས་སྒྲ་སོགས་དང་ནང་གི་རླུང་འགྲོ་འོང་སོགས་གང་ལ་ཡང་སེམས་རྟེན་མི་བྱ་ཞིང་།

སྔར་འདི་བྱས་འདི་བྱུང་སོགས་འདས་པ་ཡང་མི་སེམས། ཕྱིན་ཆད་འདི་བྱེད་འདི་བྱུང་ན་སོགས་མ་འོངས་པ་ཡང་མི་སྒྲོ། འཕྲལ་འདི་སྣང་འདི་འདུག་སོགས། ད་ལྟའི་རྟོག་པ་ཡང་ཡིད་ལ་མི་བྱེད་པར། ལྷོད་དེ་ལམ་མེ་ཐལ་ལེ་འབོལ་ལེ་གནས་སུ་བཙུག། གནས་བཞིན་ལས་ཤིགས་བཤིགས་ལ་སླར་གོང་བཞིན་བྱ། ཡུན་མི་རིང་ཙམ་ལ་གྲངས་མང་དུ་བྱའོ།།

If your attention is scattered, unresolved and you have no sense of calm, exclaim the forceful sound of PHAT or make a vigorous shout. Right then, the previous thought is interrupted and the next has not yet arisen. The attention in this gap is a thoughtfree state of calm.

Next, understand clearly that notions such as "this needs to be done to that" are thought projections. Using various methods, skillfully proceed by alternating between being focused and relaxed. Be self-confident. Persevere in the training, since by doing so you will discover the state of calm.

Shamatha without Breathing Practice

When you have achieved some degree of mental calm by the previous method, assume the same body posture as before. Do not place your attention on external visual objects, sounds or the like, nor on the inward and outward movement of the breath. Do not think about the past, what you did or what happened previously. Do not think about the future, what you will do or what will happen later. Also do not create thoughts about the present, about what appears or what is happening right now. Rather, allow yourself to remain relaxed and clear, lucid and at ease. While remaining that way, interrupt the practice. Then continue again as before. Do not maintain this too long at a time; instead repeat it many times.

In all instances of pursuing a state of calm, doing so with too much concentration and intensity may create a

གནས་ཆ་ཚོལ་བའི་རིགས་ཐམས་ཅད་ལ་ཧ་ཅང་སྒྲིམ་པ་དང་ཧུར་ཕྱུངས་དྲག་ན་སེམས་ལམ་མེར་གནས་པའི་གེགས་སུ་འགྱུར་བས་ཐལ་ཆེར་ལ་ཁོང་གློད་པ་བདེའོ།།

དེ་ལྟར་བཞག་པས་སེམས་རྒོད་པའམ་ཡེར་ན། དྲོ་སར་བསྡད་བཟའ་བཏུང་བཅུད་ཅན་བསྟེན་བསྐུ་མཉེ་བྱ་ལྟ་སྟངས་སྨད།

སེམས་ལྟེ་བའི་འོག་ཏུ་གཏད་ལ་ཕོ་རླུང་དྲག་པོ་མནན་ནོ།།

སེམས་བྱིང་བའམ་ཉོག་ན། བསིལ་སར་བསྡད་གདོང་ལ་ཆུ་ཟིལ་བཏབ་རླུང་རོ་བསལ་ལྟ་སྟངས་དཔངས་བསྟོད།

སེམས་ངར་བསྐྱེད་ལ་ཧུར་ཕྱུང་། ད་དུང་བྱིང་ན་འགྲོ་འཆག་བྱ་ཞིང་ཁམས་བསེང་ངོ་།

རླུགས་ཤིང་གཉི་སྨུག་ན། ལུས་ཁྲིད་པར་ཅན་ལ་ཕྲུག་དང་སྒོར་བ་བྱ།

མཆོད་སྦྱིན་དང་སྡིག་བཤགས་སོགས་དྲག་ཏུ་བྱ། ཏིང་ངེ་འཛིན་སྐྱེ་བར་གསོལ་བ་དུང་དུང་བཏབ་སྐྱེ་ཉམས་བསྐྱང་དུ་བཅུག།

འདི་ལ་སེམས་ཟིན་པ་བརྟན་པར་བྱེད་པ་ཞེས་བྱ་སྟེ། གནས་ཆ་རྙེད་པ་དེ་རྗེན་གཏད་མེད་དུ་འཇོག་པ་ལ་བདེ་བར་མ་བྱུང་ན་མཚན་མེད་ལ་བོགས་མི་འབྱུང་བས་བྱུང་བ་གལ་ཆེ།

དེ་ཡང་དྲན་མེད་དུ་སོང་བའི་གནས་པ་ལྷེམས་པོ་ཤར་ན་སྐྱོན་ཅན་ཡིན་པས་ཧུར་ཕྱུང་ལ་ཡུན་ཐུང་དུ་རེ་ཡང་ཡང་བསྐྱར།

hindrance for remaining lucidly attentive. For the most part, it is more suitable simply to relax.

When placing your attention in this manner, if you become agitated or scattered, sit in a warmer place, take more nutritious food and drink, do massage and lower your gaze. Focus your attention below the navel and suppress the breath in the belly with some force.

If your mind feels dull and sluggish, sit in a cooler place, splash water on your face, expel the stale breath and lift your gaze. Invigorate your attention with sharp alertness. If you still feel drowsy, refresh yourself by moving about.

If you feel obscured and stupid, bow down before sacred objects and walk around them. Make offerings and give alms, apologize for misdeeds, and so forth with deep-felt sincerity. Make yearning prayers that samadhi may arise within you. Then continue the practice.

These steps are known as *stabilizing the captured mind*. Unless you become trained so that your acquired calm can easily settle free from support and reference point, you will not find any enhancement in the practice without attributes. Training is therefore essential.

It is an error to let your sense of calm become absent-minded or numb, so be on the alert and continue by repeated short periods.

If you feel sluggish or dull, with just the barest presence of mind, you must energetically purge this shortcoming, so train exclusively in purifying that for a while. Alter-

བྱིང་བའམ་ལྷོད་བ་བེ་བ་དྲན་རིག་ཡོད་པ་ཙམ་བྱུང་ན་སྐྱོན་ཤུགས་ཀྱིས་དག་འགྲོ་བས་རེ་ཞིག་དེ་ཉིད་རང་སྐྱུང་བའམ། སེམས་རྒྱུད་ཟད་དར་བསྐྱེད་ལ་སྐྱུང་བ་གང་འཕྲོད་བྱེད་དུ་བཅུག་གོ།།

གཉིས་པ་མཚན་མེད་ལ་གཉིས།

སྒྲིམ་པ་དང་། གློད་པའོ།།

དང་པོ་ནི། ལུས་གནད་སྔར་ལྟར་ལས་ལྟ་སྟངས་མིག་རང་གི་ཐད་ཀར་གཏད།

སེམས་དར་བསྐྱེད་ནས་སྐད་ཅིག་ཀྱང་མ་ཡེངས་པར་བསྒྲིམས་ཏེ། འདི་སྒོམ་གྱི་དམིགས་གཏད་མེད་པར་རྩེ་གཅིག་ཏུ་སིང་ངེ་ཡེ་རེ་བཞག།

ཡུན་མི་རིང་ཙམ་ལ་བཞིག་ནས་ཡང་གྲིམ་གྱིས་བསྒྲིམས་ལ་སྐད་ཅིག་ཀྱང་མ་ཡེངས་པར་ཅེན་ནེ་འཇོག་པ་ལ་སྐྱུང་དུ་བཅུག་ལ་ཉམས་ལྟ་བྱས་པས།

སྔར་གྱི་གནས་པ་སྒོམ་མེ་བ་ལས་སེམས་དྭང་སོང་ངེ་ནས་གསལ་ལེ་སིང་ངེ་གནས་ཤིང་དྲན་རིག་ཡེ་རེ་འདུག་ན་བོགས་ཐོན་པ་ཡིན་ལ།

བློ་རྟོད་པའི་རིགས་འགའ་ལ་དྭང་ཆ་ཐོན་ཡང་གནས་ཡུན་ཐུང་དུ་སོང་ན་སྐྱོན་དུ་མི་བཟུང་བར་ཡུན་ཐུང་གྲངས་མང་བྱས་པས་གནས་པ་དྭང་པོ་འཕེལ་ནས་འོང་ངོ་།།

nately, you can train while generating a slight sharpness of attention. Use whichever method feels more suitable.

Shamatha without Attributes

This has two points:

Tightening
Loosening

Tightening

Keep the same posture as before but raise your gaze a little higher and aim it at the level directly before you. Sharpen your attention and focus so as not to be distracted for even a second. Remain one-pointedly clear and lucid without the reference point of something particular to be cultivated by meditating.

After a while, break up (the meditation); keep it short. Again scrupulously focus yourself. Remain with a sense of precision that does not wander off for even an instant. Train like this and gain some personal experience.

By doing so, rather than the previous dull type of calm, your mind brightens up and becomes clear and lucid. You have gained progress when your mindful presence is lucidly clear.

Some people of the quick-witted type may find that they do brighten up, but the periods of being calm become shorter. Do not regard that as a fault. Continue training in short periods many times, and by doing so both the calm and the lucidity will expand.

གཉིས་པ་ནི། ལུས་གནད་དང་ལྟ་སྟངས་གོང་བཞིན་བྱ་འདི་སྒོམ་འདི་མི་སྒོམ་དང་གནས་ན་དགའ་འགྲོ་ན་མི་དགའ་བ་ལ་སོགས་པའི་ཞེ་འདོད་མ་བྱས་པར་སེམས་ལྷོད་གློད་ལ། དགག་སྒྲུབ་དང་བཅས་བཅོས་མ་བྱས་པར་སེམས་རང་བབས་སུ་འབོལ་ལེ་ཆམ་མེ་བཞག་ཅིང་། དེའི་ངང་ནས་མ་ཡེངས་ཙམ་གྱི་དྲན་པ་ཕྱུར་ཕྱུར་མིན་པའི་སྐབས་ཆེ་བ་ས་ལེ་བ་བྱས་ལ་གུ་ཡངས་སང་ངེ་བསྐྱང་ངོ་།

དེ་ལྟར་བསྐྱངས་པས་རྣམ་རྟོག་རགས་པ་ཧིལ་གྱིས་འཆར་ན་དགག་ཀྱང་མི་དགག་རྗེས་སུ་ཡང་མི་འབྲང་བར་མ་ཡེངས་པའི་དྲན་པ་རང་ཚོ་བཟུང་།

འགྱུ་བ་སན་ཐུན་ཕྲ་སེམ་མེ་བ་རྣམས་ལའང་དགག་སྒྲུབ་མི་བྱ། དྭང་མ་སིང་ངེ་ལྷན་ནེ་གནས་པ་དང་ཤིགས་བཤིགས་ལ་ཅུང་ཟད་རེ་ངལ་གསོ།

ཡང་སྔར་བཞིན་བསྐྱང་དུ་བཅུག་ལ་ཉམས་བལྟ། དེ་ལ་སྔར་རྣམ་རྟོག་ཕྲ་རགས་རྣམས་བཀག་པ་ལྟར་བྱས་ཏེ་རིག་པ་སིང་ངེ་ཡོ་རེ་བར་བཅོས་ནས་སེམས་རྩེ་གཅིག་ཏུ་བསྒྲིམ་དགོས་པ་ལྟ་བུས་ཅུང་ཟད་མི་བདེ་ལ།

འདིར་མ་ཡེངས་ཙམ་གྱི་ངང་ནས་རང་ལུགས་སུ་བསྐྱང་བས་ཆོག་པ་དང་རྣམ་རྟོག་ཕྲ་རགས་འཆར་ན་ཡང་དྲན་པའི་ཚེ་བཟུང་བས་རྣམ་རྟོག་གིས་དོན་བྱེད་མི་ནུས་པར་ལྷན་གྱིས་ཞི་ནས་གནས་པའི་སྟེང་དུ་འགྲོ་བ་དང་།

Loosening

Take the same posture and keep the same gaze as above. Do not entertain any ambitions about what should or should not be cultivated by meditating. Do not be happy when calm or unhappy when thoughts move; rather, relax your attention loosely. Do not inhibit one thing while promoting another. Do not make adjustments. Leave your attention as it naturally is — relaxed and free. From within this state, maintain a presence of mind that is simply not distracted. Do not fidget; be expansive and clear. Train in being open and vividly present.

While training in this way, when an obtrusive thought intrudes, you need neither begin to block it nor pursue it. Rather, maintain a steady and unwavering presence of mind.

Nor do you need to block off or encourage the subtle fluttering of thoughts. Remain clear, lucid and quiet. Then interrupt to take a short break. Once again, continue training as before to see what experience you gain.

Formerly, you had to focus one-pointedly by fashioning your conscious mind into being clear and open, while almost repressing coarse and subtle thoughts. This was somewhat uneasy (to sustain). So now, instead, it is enough to sustain the natural way of simply being undistracted.

When thoughts do occur, be they coarse or subtle, embrace them with mindful presence. By doing so, thoughts are unable to function as thoughts. They completely subside and you arrive in a state of calm.

དྲན་པས་ཁྲིབ་ན་གཞན་ཞེ་འདོད་མི་དགོས་པས་གྲུ་ཡངས་པ་ལྟ་བུ་ཞིག་འབྱུང་བ་དང་། ཤིགས་བཤིག་ལྷོད་གློད་དུས་སེམས་ཀྱང་ཤིག་གེ་ལྷོད་དེ་གནས་པའི་མཚང་རིག་ནས་སྐྱོང་བདེ་ན་བོགས་ཐོན་པ་ཡིན་ཞིང་།

གལ་ཏེ་འོག་འགྲུ་ལྟ་བུར་ཤོར་ནས་ཡེངས་པའམ།

ཅི་འགྲུས་འདི་འགྲུས་མེད་པར་དྲན་མེད་དུ་ཡེངས་པ་སོགས་བྱུང་ན་དྲན་པ་སྟོབས་ཆུང་བ་ཡིན་ལ།

གནས་པ་སན་ནེ་བ་བྲང་ངེ་བ་འཚུབ་བེ་བ་བྱུང་ན་གློད་ཞན་པ་དང་དྲན་རིག་ཕྱུར་བ་ཡིན་པས་སྐྱོང་ལུགས་ཀྱིས་སྐྱོན་བསལ་ཏེ་སྐྱོང་དུ་བཅུག།

བློ་རིགས་བྱིང་ན་དྲན་རིག་གི་ངར་དང་སྟོབས་བསྐྱེད།

རྒོད་ན་སེམས་ངར་ཅུང་ཟད་སླད་དེ་གློད་ཆ་ཆེར་བཏང་ལ་བསྒྱུངས་པས་སེམས་གསལ་སེང་ངེ་གནས་ཤིང་།

གཟུགས་སྒྲ་སོགས་ཀྱི་སྣང་བ་ཡང་ཞ་ལེ་བ་ཆམ་མེ་བ་སོང་ངེ་བ་བུན་ནེ་བ་ལྟ་བུར་འཆར་ན་ཞི་གནས་སྐྱེས་པ་ཡིན་པས།

ཉམས་ཀྱི་བྱེ་བྲག་ཅི་འཆར་ནའང་དེའི་དབང་དུ་མི་འབྲང་བར་གསལ་སེང་ངེ་བ་ལ་མི་རྟོག་པའི་ངང་དུ་རེ་ཞིག་བསྒོམ་དུ་བཅུག།

འདིར་རྐང་མ་ཚུགས་ན་སྒོམ་ཉིན་སྲིབ་ཅན་འོང་བས་རྐང་ཚུགས་པར་བྱ་སྟེ།

Once you have embraced a thought with this presence of mind, you need not keep any other aim, so you get a sense of feeling very free. During this type of release and relaxation, you appreciate the vital point of remaining in a free and easy state of mind. You have gained progress once this has become simple to sustain.

However, if you get distracted while lost in the undercurrent of thought or carried away mindlessly without noticing what you are thinking of, then your presence of mind is too weak.

If your calm feels restless, unsettled or fidgety, your sense of looseness is inadequate or you are too intensely mindful. Clear up these shortcomings and continue the training.

If the attention feels dull, develop a more vigorous mindful presence. If agitated, slightly lessen its strength to deepen the relaxed quality. By continuing in this way, your attention will remain utterly lucid.

Shamatha has taken birth when perceptions of sights, sounds and so forth are experienced as vivid and serene, lucid and unbound. So, even if one of the various meditation-moods do occur, do not get caught up in it. Instead, train for a while in the state that is both lucid and thoughtfree.

Unless you get a firm footing in this, your meditation training will become sporadic. Gain a steadfast foothold.

དང་པོར་རྣམ་རྟོག་ཕྲ་རགས་མང་པོ་འཁྲུགས་པའི་བར་ན་མི་རྟོག་པར་གནས་པའི་ཆ་ཙུང་ཟད་ཙམ་རེ་སྐྱེད་པ་དེ་གཅོང་རོང་གི་འབབ་ཆུ་འདྲ་བའི་ཞི་གནས་དང་པོ་ཡིན།

དེ་ནས་རྣམ་རྟོག་ཕལ་ཆེར་ཕྲ་ཉལ་གྱིས་སོང་ཞི་གནས་བདེ་ཆམ་མེ་གནས་ཞིང་། འོན་ཀྱང་རྣམ་རྟོག་གི་གཡོ་བ་དྲག་པོ་བྱུང་ན་མི་ནོན་པར་སྐབས་སྐབས་འཕྲོ་རྒོད་འབྱུང་བ་དེ་ཆུ་བོ་དལ་ཞིང་གཡོ་བ་ལྟ་བུའི་ཞི་གནས་བར་པ་ཡིན།

དེ་ནས་རྣམ་རྟོག་ཕྲ་རགས་མི་ལྡང་བར་མི་རྟོག་པའི་ངང་དུ་བདེ་མེ་རེ་ཙེ་ཙམ་བཞག་གི་བར་གནས་པའམ། རྣམ་རྟོག་ཕྲ་མོ་ཙུང་ཟད་རེ་ལྡང་ན་ཡང་དེས་རྟོག་པའི་བྱ་བ་མི་ནུས་པར་མི་རྟོག་པའི་ངང་དུ་རང་སར་དག་པ་དེ་ཆུ་མ་བུ་འཕྲད་པ་རྒྱ་མཚོ་ལྟ་བུའི་ཞི་གནས་མཐར་ཐུག་ཡིན་པས།

ཞི་གནས་འདིས་ཕྱག་རྒྱ་ཆེན་པོའི་སྒོམ་ངོ་བོའི་གོ་མི་ཆོད་ན་ཡང་སྒོམ་གྱི་གཞི་ལ་ཡོད་པ་ཤིན་ཏུ་གལ་ཆེ་ཞིང་།

རྣམ་དཀར་གྱི་ལས་གསོག་པའི་བསམ་གཏན་ཚད་མེད་པ་ཞིག་ཡིན་པས་ཞི་གནས་སྐྱོན་མེད་བརྟན་པོ་བསྒྲུབ་པར་བྱའོ།

༈ གཉིས་པ་ལྷག་མཐོང་གི་སྒོ་ནས་ཁྲིད་པས་གཉིས།

སེམས་སྣང་སྣ་ཚོགས་ཀྱི་ངོ་བོ་གཏན་ལ་དབབ་པ་དང་།

གཞི་རྩལ་སྒྲོ་འདོགས་བཅད་པའོ།།

At the beginning, you gain a slight degree of thought-free calm amidst the turbulence of the many gross and subtle thoughts. This is the first stage of shamatha, similar to a mountain stream rolling through a gorge.

Next, the thinking, for the most part, vanishes; so that your shamatha state remains serenely blissful. However, whenever a strong movement of thought occurs you are unable to keep it down. From time to time you get involved in being scattered and agitated. This is the intermediate stage of shamatha, similar to the placid flow of a river.

Then, both coarse and subtle thoughts no longer arise. As long as you compose yourself in this thoughtfree state, you can remain serenely blissful. Even if a remnant of a subtle thought arises, it is unable to function as an actual thought; rather, it naturally dissolves into a state of nonthought. This is the ultimate stage of shamatha, like the mother ocean meeting its river child.

Even though this type of shamatha does not suffice as the real substance of Mahamudra training, it is extremely important to have it as the basis for the training. Since it is mental stability that creates boundless virtuous karma, you should accomplish a flawless and steady state of shamatha.

Guiding by Means of Vipashyana

This has two parts:

Establishing the identity of mind and the various perceptions
Clearing up uncertainties about basis and expression

དང་པོ་ལ་གཉིས། རྒྱུ་བ་སེམས་ཀྱི་ངོ་བོ་གཏན་ལ་དབབ་པ་དང་།

རྒྱུ་ལ་རྣམ་རྟོག་དང་སྣང་བའི་ངོ་བོ་གཏན་ལ་དབབ་པའོ།།

དང་པོ་ནི། ལུས་གནད་སྔར་བཞིན་ལས་མིག་ཚམ་ཚུམ་དང་འགྱུར་བ་མེད་པར་ཧར་རེ་གཏད།

ཤེས་པ་གསལ་སིང་ངེ་བ་ལ་མི་རྟོག་པའི་ཞི་གནས་ཀྱི་སྟེང་དུ་ལྷང་ངེ་བཞག་ལ། དེའི་ངང་ལ་སེམས་དེ་ཉིད་ལ་རྗེན་ལྷང་གིས་བལྟས་ཏེ་དབྱིབས་དང་ཁ་དོག་ལ་སོགས་པ་ཇི་ལྟ་བུ་ཞིག་འདུག།

གནས་དང་རྟེན་གང་ལ་གནས། ངོས་བཟུང་རྣམ་འགྱུར་ཇི་ལྟར་འདུག་རྣམས་རིམ་པས་བརྟགས་ཤིང་དཔྱད།

དེ་ཡང་ཟླུམ་པོ་གྲུ་བཞི་སོགས་དང་ས་རྗེ་རི་བྲག་རྩེ་ཞིང་སོགས་དང་མི་དང་དུད་འགྲོ་སོགས་ཀྱི་དབྱིབས་སུ་འདུག་གམ།

དཀར་པོ་དང་ནག་པོ་སོགས་ཀྱི་ཁ་དོག་ཏུ་འདུག་གམ།

རེ་རེ་ཞིང་རྗེ་རྩུས་འཕྲོད་པར་བརྟག།

དེ་བཞིན་དུ་སེམས་ཕྱི་རོལ་སྣོད་བཅུད་ཀྱི་དངོས་པོ་ལ་གནས་སམ་ནང་རྣམ་སྨིན་གྱི་ལུས་ལ་གནས།

Establishing the Identity of Mind and the Various Perceptions

This has two points:

Establishing the identity of mind — the basis

Establishing the identity of thoughts and perceptions — the expression

Establishing the Identity of Mind — the Basis

For the first point, assume the same body posture as before. In addition, gaze straight ahead without blinking or shifting. Keep your attention vividly present in the thoughtfree and lucid state of shamatha. During this state, look directly into this attentive mind to see what shape, color, etc. it has. In which location does it remain and what supports it? What kind of definable identity and appearance does it have? Gradually examine and investigate these points.

In other words, does it have a shape that is round, square or the like? Does it have a shape like the earth, rocks, mountains, scrubs, trees or the like? Does it have a shape that looks like a human being, an animal or what? Does it have a color such as white or black, etc.? Examine each instance until you reach a definite conclusion.

In the same way, examine whether the mind lives in external things of the world or beings, or in your body of karmic ripening. If it does live in this body, does it remain in a particular location or part of the body, from the crown of the head to the soles of your feet, or does it remain in a pervasive way? If it remains in a pervasive way,

ལུས་ལ་གནས་ན་སྐྱི་གཙུག་ནས་རྐང་མཐིལ་གྱི་བར་ལྷུ་དང་དུམ་བུ་ལ་གནས་སམ་སྐྱི་ཁྲབ་ཏུ་གནས། སྐྱི་ཁྲབ་ཏུ་གནས་ན་ཕྱི་ནང་གི་ཚུལ་དུ་གནས་སམ་འདྲེས་པའི་ཚུལ་དུ་གནས། འདྲེས་ན་སེམས་ཕྱིའི་ཡུལ་དང་རྫས་ལ་འཕྲོས་པའི་ཚེ་ཇི་ལྟར་སོང་ལ་སོགས་པ་བརྟག། དེ་བཞིན་དུ་སེམས་ཀྱི་ངོ་བོ་དེ་སྟོང་པའི་ངོས་བཟུང་དུ་འདུག་གམ་གསལ་བའི་ངོས་བཟུང་དུ་འདུག། སྟོང་པ་ལ་ཅང་མེད་ཀྱི་སྟོང་པའམ་ནམ་མཁའ་ལྟ་བུའི་སྟོང་པར་འདུག་དང་། གསལ་རིག་ཅན་ལ་ཉི་ཟླའི་འོད་དམ་མར་མེ་ལྟ་བུ་སོགས་ཇི་ལྟར་གསལ་བརྟག་ཏུ་བཅུག། འདི་ལ་ཇོ་ནུས་ཐུག་པ་ཁོ་ཐག་མ་ཆོད་ཀྱི་བར་བརྟག་དཔྱད་བྱ། ཐོས་ལོ་དང་གོ་བ་ཙམ་ཞེ་ལ་བཞག་ནས་མ་བརྟགས་ན་ཞུག་ཐག་མི་ཆོད་པས་ཞུགས་གཏུག་ལ་བརྟག་ཏུ་བཅུག།

ལོག་ཤེས་བཟུང་ན་གནོད་བྱེད་བདུད་ལ་སླར་གཞིག་ཏུ་བཅུག་པས་དབྱིབས་དང་ཁ་དོག་དང་གནས་དང་རྟེན་དང་རྫས་སུ་མ་གྲུབ་པར་ཐག་ཆོད་པ་ནི་སླ་ལ། ངོ་བོ་ངོས་བཟུང་གསལ་སྟོང་གི་ངང་དུ་ལྷན་ནེ་གནས་པ་ཞིག་ཏུ་གོ་ན་གནས་པའི་ཉམས་ཡིན་པའི་འཕྲིག་མ་ཆུད་པས།

མཏྲལ་དང་གསོལ་བ་དྲག་ཏུ་འདེབས་ཤིང་གསལ་ལུགས་དང་སྟོང་ལུགས་གནས་ལུགས་རྣམས་རེ་རེ་ཞིང་བརྟག་ཏུ་བཅུག་པས།

དངོས་པོ་དང་རྫས་སུ་མ་གྲུབ་པས་དབྱིབས་དང་ཁ་དོག་མེད་ཅིང་གནས་དང་རྟེན་ཡང་མེད་ལ།

does it dwell in a way that has an inside and an outside, or does it remain in a way that is diffuse? If diffuse, examine how your mind moves and so forth when becoming occupied by outer objects and things.

Likewise, is your mind an entity that can be identified as empty or as aware?[4] Regarding the empty quality, does that mean being empty like nothingness or empty like space? Is the lucidly aware quality radiant like the light of the sun and moon, or like the flame of a butter lamp? Examine what this lucidity is like. Investigate this until it is settled with complete and conclusive certainty.

If you hold on to hearsay and theory and neglect investigating, you will not feel it is conclusively decided. So examine this to the very depth.

If an incorrect understanding is held, counter-arguments should be applied and the investigation continued.

❧

It is easy to resolve that (this conscious mind) does not consist of any shape, color, location, support or material substance. However, if you take it to be a definable entity that is aware and empty and you remain quietly in that state, you are still unresolved, since that is the meditative mood of stillness. Therefore, make mandala offerings, supplicate with deep devotion and investigate each instance of how it is aware, how it is empty and what its real mode is.

Through this you may find that mind is not comprised of a concrete or material substance and therefore has no shape or color, no dwelling place or support. You may also

འདི་འདྲ་འདི་ཡིན་གྱི་ངོས་བཟུང་མེད་པར་གསལ་སྟོང་ལྷ་སྦུའི་བརྗོད་མི་ཚུགས་པ་ཅིག་ལ་སྒྲོང་རྒྱུ་ཡོད་པ་ཅིག་ཏུ་གོ་ན།

མགོ་གཡོགས་ལ་གཙུན་པས་གོ་བའམ་རྣ་ཐོས་ཡིན་ན་མི་མཚུངས་པ་མང་པོ་འབྱུང་ཞིང་རྟག་མི་ཐུབ། སྒྲོང་བ་ཡིན་ན་ཟེར་ལུགས་མི་ཤེས་ནའང་གོ་དོན་ཐག་གཅིག་ཏུ་འོང་། དེ་བྱུང་ན་སྒྲོང་བ་སྐྱེས་པ་ཡིན་ནོ།།

འོན་ཀྱང་སླ་མཁས་ཤིང་ཚིག་ལེགས་ཀྱང་སྒྲོང་བ་མེད་པ་དང་། སླ་མི་ཤེས་བཤད་མི་ཚུགས་ཀྱང་སྒྲོང་བ་སྐྱེས་པ་ཡོང་བས་བླ་མས་སྒྲོང་ཐོག་ནས་གདར་ཤ་ལེགས་པར་བཅད་ལ་ཞུ་ཐག་ཆོད་པ་དང་།

སྔར་གྱི་ཞི་གནས་གསལ་སིང་ངེ་བ་ལ་མི་རྟོག་པའི་ངང་ནས་སེམས་ལ་རྗེན་ལྷག་གིས་བལྟས་པས་ཚིག་གི་བརྗོད་པས་མི་མཚོན་པའི་ཤེས་པ།

ངོས་བཟུང་མེད་བཞིན་ཏུ་རང་རིག་པའི་གསལ་སྟོང་སིང་ངེ་བ་ཡེ་རེ་བ་རྀག་གེ་བ་ལྷ་སྦུ་དེ་མ་ཡེངས་པར་སྐྱོང་དུ་བཅུག་གོ།།

གཉིས་པ་ནི། ལུས་གནད་སོགས་གོང་ལྟར་བྱས་ཏེ་ངོས་བཟུང་མེད་པའི་སེམས་གསལ་སྟོང་གི་ངང་ནས་ཞི་སྣང་ལྷ་སྦུའི་རྣམ་རྟོག་རགས་ཤིང་ངར་ཆེ་བ་ཞིག་འགྱུར་བཅུག་ལ།

དེ་ལྟང་གིས་སྐྱེས་པ་དང་དེ་ལ་རྗེན་ཆར་གྱིས་བལྟས་ནས་དབྱིབས་དང་ཁ་དོག་གནས་དང་རྟེན་ངོས་བཟུང་དང་རྣམ་འགྱུར་སོགས་ཇི་ལྟར་འདུག་སྔར་ལྟར་བརྟག་དཔྱད་བྱ།

understand that it is an aware emptiness that defies any description of being such-and-such — it is inexpressible and yet it can be experienced.

When that is the case, the lama should try to present confusing statements. If the meditator's understanding is merely theory or hearsay it will be inconsistent and will not withstand scrutiny. If it is personal experience, it will converge on one point even when he is unable to articulate with traditional words. When this happens, the meditator has reached personal experience.

Even so, there are eloquent and articulate meditators who lack personal experience. There are also experienced and tongue-tied meditators who are unable to explain. The lama should therefore let them thoroughly investigate and resolve this fully through real experience.

While in the previous state of lucid and thoughtfree shamatha, as before, look directly into your conscious mind. It is a wakefulness for which no words suffice. It is not a definable entity,[5] but at the same time, it is a self-knowing aware emptiness that is clear, lucid and awake. Sustain this without distraction.

Establishing the Identity of Thoughts and Perceptions — the Expression

Assume the same posture as mentioned above. Now, allow a strong and coarse thought state, such as anger, to occur within the empty and aware state of unidentifiable mind. When it has vividly arisen look into it directly and investigate, just as before, its exact color and shape, its

དེ་བཞིན་དུ་རྣམ་རྟོག་ཕྲ་མོ་ཤར་བའམ་སྤྲོས་ཏེ་དེའི་ངོ་བོ་ལ་བལྟ་ཞིང་བརྟག་དཔྱད་བྱ། དེ་བཞིན་སྡོད་བཙུད་དང་དགྲ་གཉེན་དང་སྐྱིད་སྡུག་ལ་སོགས་པའི་སྣང་བའི་འཆར་སྒོ་ཕྲ་རགས་ཅི་རིགས་པ་ཤར་བའམ་འཆར་དུ་བཙུག་ལ་དེའི་ངོ་བོ་ལ་བརྟག་ཅིང་དཔྱད། སྔར་བལྟས་པས་ངོས་བཟུང་མ་བྱུང་བའི་རིགས་འགྲོ་བྱེད་ནས་མ་བརྟག་ན་སྦྱོང་བ་ཕྲ་ཞིབ་ཅན་མི་འབྱུང་ཞིང་། རྣམ་རྟོག་དང་སྣང་བ་ཕྲ་རགས་ལ་ངོས་བཟུང་མེད་པའི་གོ་བ་ཙམ་ལས་ཐུག་འཕྲོད་དུ་ངོ་ཤེས་འཕྲོད་པ་ལྟ་བུ་འམ། རྫུན་ཞུགས་རྫིབ་པ་ལྟ་བུར་གྲོལ་བའི་སྦྱོང་བ་རྒྱུན་བརྟན་པོ་མི་འོང་བས་སྙིང་རུས་བསྐྱེད་ནས་ཁོ་ཐག་མ་ཆོད་ཀྱི་བར་བརྟག་དཔྱད་བྱེད་དུ་བཙུག་གོ།།

འདིས་བློ་གཅོད་ཁམས་བཟང་ངན་ཤུ་ལ་ཡང་དོན་གྱི་ཐོབ་པ་ཆེན་པོ་འབྱུང་བས་འོལ་གསལ་སྤྱི་ཙམ་ལ་མི་བཞག་གོ།།

དེ་ནས་ཉམས་བལྟས་པས། རྣམ་རྟོག་གང་སྣང་བའི་འཆར་སྒོ་རྣམས་བརྟགས་པའི་ཚེ་དབྱིབས་ཁ་དོག་དང་ངོས་བཟུང་མི་འདུག་ཅིང་། སེམས་ཀྱི་ངོ་བོ་གསལ་སྟོང་དེ་ཀར་སོང་ཞེས་པ་ལ་སོགས་པའི་གོ་ཡུལ་ཙམ་ཟེར་ན།

གསལ་སྟོང་ཟེར་བའི་ཚིགས་རིགས་ལ་ངེས་པ་མེད་པས་རྣམ་རྟོག་ལ་སོགས་པའི་འཆར་སྒོ་དེ་འགག་པའམ་ཞིག་པ་ལྟ་བུ་མེད་པར་གསལ་སྟོང་དུ་སོང་ངམ།

location and support, its identity and appearance, and so forth. In the same way, let a subtle thought state arise or project one, and then look into and examine its identity.

Similarly, let arise or produce a variety of subtle and coarse perceptions — of the world and its beings, enemies and friends, joys and sorrows, and so forth. Look into the identity of each. Scrutinize and examine it.

Before, when you looked, perhaps you did so by generalizing the lack of definable entity, or you didn't examine and failed to gain a precise experience. If so, you have only gained the theory that subtle and coarse thoughts and perceptions are unidentifiable. You will therefore not have found the ongoing and steady experience of liberation which is to be able to recognize directly their identity upon encountering them or to let their falsehood collapse. Therefore, don the armor of fortitude and continue examining until you have settled this point decisively.

By doing this, a profound certainty will be attained, whether one is of a higher or lower acumen. This topic should therefore not be left vague or as a general idea.

Next, in order to continue to gain personal experience, examine a particular thought or perception. You may now say, "It does not have any shape, color or definable identity. The identity of mind is simply an aware emptiness!" Or you may deliver some other piece of theoretical understanding.

However, it isn't certain what you mean by *aware emptiness*. Do you mean an aware emptiness that happens after

ཡོད་བཞིན་དུ་ནི་གསལ་བ་ཡིན་དུ་ཆུག་ཀྱང་སྟོང་པའི་དོན་མེད་དོ་ཞེས་གཙུན་ལ་བརྟག་དཔྱད་བྱེད་དུ་བཙུག།

རྣམ་རྟོག་གང་ཤར་དེའི་འཆར་སྒོ་དེ་ཉིད་མ་འགགས་པར་གསལ་བཞིན་དུ་རྟོག་པའི་བྱ་བ་མི་བྱེད་པའི་ངོས་བཟུང་རྒྱུ་མེད་པ་ཞིག་དང་།

སྣང་བ་ཡང་སྣང་ཆམ་འགག་པར་སྣང་ཙམ་ལས་ཨ་འཐས་ཀྱི་བདེན་འཛིན་མེད་པ་བཀྲག་མེད་ལྷ་བུ་འདི་འདྲ་ཞེས་བརྗོད་པར་དཀའ་བ་ཞིག་འདུག་པར་གོ་ནས་མྱོང་བ་སྐྱེས་པ་ཡིན་པས།

གསལ་ལ་ངོས་བཟུང་མེད་པ་གསལ་སྟོང་ངམ་སྣང་ལ་རང་བཞིན་མེད་པ་སྣང་སྟོང་དེ་ཉིད་རང་མ་ཡེངས་པར་སྐྱོང་དུ་བཙུག།

ཁ་ཅིག་རྣམ་རྟོག་གམ་སྣང་བ་ལ་ཅེར་བལྟས་པས་དེ་ཞིག་ནས་གསལ་སྟོང་དུ་འགྲོ་ཟེར་བ་ནི་རྟོག་པ་དང་སྣང་བ་ཉིད་གདན་ལ་མ་ཕེབས་པར་དེའི་གཉེན་པོར་གསལ་སྟོང་གི་བློ་བཏང་བའོ།།

གཉིས་པ་ལ་བཞི།

རྣམ་རྟོག་སེམས་སུ་ཐག་བཅད་པ།

སྣང་བ་སེམས་སུ་ཐག་བཅད་པ།

a thought event has ceased or dissolved? Or is it an aware emptiness while the thought is present? In the latter case, you may say the state is aware, but it is meaningless to say it is empty. Scrutinize in this way and continue examining.

No matter what kind of thought occurs, its experience is, in itself, something unidentifiable — it is unobstructedly aware and yet not conceptualizing. As for perceptions, they are a mere impression of unobstructed presence, which is insubstantial and not a clinging to a solid reality. They are hard to describe as being such-and-such, and when you understand them to be this way you have reached personal experience.

Without getting distracted then, simply sustain this aware emptiness that is an unidentifiable awareness, also referred to as a perceiving emptiness that is perception devoid of a self-nature.

Someone may say, "When I look directly into a thought or perception, it dissolves and becomes an aware emptiness." This is a case of not having established certainty about the nature of thoughts and perceptions, but rather of using the idea of aware emptiness as an antidote against them.

Clearing Up Uncertainties About Basis and Expression

This has four points:

Resolving that thoughts are mind

Resolving that perceptions are mind

སེམས་གནས་འགྲུའི་རྩ་བ་བཅད་པ།

གང་ཤར་སྐྱེ་མེད་དུ་ཐག་བཅད་པའོ།།

དང་པོ་ནི། ལུས་གནད་སོགས་སྔར་ལྟར་བྱས་ལ་སེམས་གསལ་སྟོང་དུ་མཉམ་པར་བཞག་པའི་ངང་ནས་ཞེ་སྡང་ལ་སོགས་པའི་རྣམ་རྟོག་ཅིག་ལམ་གྱིས་སྤྲོས་ཏེ། དེ་ལ་ཅེར་གྱིས་བལྟས་ལ་དེ་རྒྱུའམ་གཞི་ཅི་ལ་བརྟེན་ནས་བྱུང་ལེགས་པར་བརྟག།

སེམས་གསལ་སྟོང་གི་ངང་དེ་ཉིད་ལས་བྱུང་སྙམ་ན། མ་ལས་བུ་སྐྱེས་པ་ལྟར་བྱུང་ངམ་ཉི་མ་ལས་འོད་ཤར་བ་ལྟར་རམ་སེམས་དེ་རྣམ་རྟོག་དེར་སོང་ལ་སོགས་པ་བརྟག།

ཚུལ་ཇི་ལྟ་བུར་གནས་བལྟས་ལ་ཞེ་སྡང་གི་རྣམ་པར་སྣང་ན། ཞེ་སྡང་དེ་ཉིད་ཀུན་དཀྲིས་དྲག་པོའི་བདེན་འཛིན་དང་བཅས་པར་སྣང་ངམ། ཞེ་སྡང་ལྟ་བུའི་རྣམ་པ་ཙམ་ལ་ངོ་བོ་ངོས་བཟུང་རྒྱུ་མེད་པའི་ཕྱལ་ལེ་བ་ལྟ་བུ་ཞིག་འདུག་བརྟག། མཐར་ཇི་ལྟར་སོང་བལྟས་ལ་རྟོག་པ་དེ་བཀག་གམ་སངས། བཀག་ན་སུས་བཀག་རྐྱེན་ཅིས་དགགས། སངས་ན་རྐྱེན་གྱིས་སངས་སམ་རང་སངས་ལ་སོང་བ་བརྟག།

དེ་བཞིན་དུ་རྣམ་རྟོག་ཕྲ་རགས་སྣ་ཚོགས་པ་ལ་གོང་བཞིན་བརྟག་དཔྱད་བྱེད་དུ་བཅུག་ལ་ཉམས་བལྟ། ལོག་ཤེས་འདུག་ན་གནོད་བྱེད་བཏང་ཞིང་ཕྱོགས་ཙམ་བསྟན་ལ་སླར་བརྟག་དུ་བཅུག།

Investigating the calm and the moving mind
Resolving that all experience is nonarising

Resolving That Thoughts Are Mind

Assume the same posture as before. Let your mind be evenly composed as aware emptiness. From within this state project a vivid thought, such as anger. Look directly into it and thoroughly investigate from what kind of substance or basis it arose.

Perhaps you suppose that it arose from this state of empty and aware mind itself. If so, examine whether it is like a child born from its mother or like light shining from the sun. Or is it the mind that becomes the thought?

Next, observe the way in which it remains. When it appears in the form of anger, examine whether this anger is accompanied by the fetter of intense clinging to things as being real or whether it is simply an appearance of anger, an openness in which there is no identity to take hold of.

Finally, observe how a thought departs. Is the thought stopped or does it dissolve? If it is stopped, who stopped it or what circumstance made it stop? If it dissolves, examine whether it dissolves due to some circumstance or whether it dissolves by itself.

In the same way, a variety of gross and subtle thoughts should be examined to gain some experience. If the meditator holds a wrong understanding, it should be eliminated with a counter-argument and a hint given. After that, the meditator should once more continue examining.

འདི་ན་འདི་བཞིན་བྱུང་དང་དབྱིབས་རྣམ་འགྱུར་འདིར་གནས་དང་ཐ་མ་འདིར་སོང་མི་རྙེད་ཀྱང་རྣམ་རྟོག་དང་སེམས་ཐ་དད་དང་ཕྱི་ནང་ལྟ་བུ་དང་ལུས་དང་ཡན་ལག་ལྟ་བུའི་བློ་ཞིག་ནས།

རྣམ་རྟོག་སྣ་ཚོགས་པ་རྣམ་པ་ཅིར་སྣང་ཡང་ངོ་བོ་ངོས་བཟུང་མེད་པ་སྣང་སྟོང་དུ་སྤྱོད་ཞིང་རང་ཤར་རང་གྲོལ་དུ་རིག་སྟེ།

སེམས་ཀྱི་གོ་མ་འགག་པས་སེམས་རྣམ་རྟོག་ཏུ་ཤར་བའམ་དེར་སྣང་བ་ཙམ་དུ་ངེས་ནས་རྣམ་རྟོག་དང་སེམས་ཉིད་དབྱེར་མེད་དུ་ཐག་ཆོད་དགོས་ལ།

དཔེར་ན་ཆུའི་རླབས་ལྟ་བུ་སྟེ། རླབས་ནི་ཆུ་ལས་མ་འདས་ཤིང་ཆུ་ཉིད་ཀྱང་རླབས་སུ་ཤར་ལ། ཤར་ཡང་ཆུའི་རང་བཞིན་ལས་མ་གཡོས་པ་ལྟར།

རྣམ་རྟོག་སྣ་ཚོགས་པ་ཤར་ཙམ་ཉིད་ནས་ངོས་བཟུང་མེད་པའི་སེམས་གསལ་སྟོང་ལས་མ་འདས་ཤིང་། སེམས་ཀྱང་འཆར་སྒོ་མ་འགག་པས་རྣམ་རྟོག་སྣ་ཚོགས་པ་ཤར་ལ།

དེར་ཤར་ཡང་ངོ་བོ་ངོས་བཟུང་མེད་པའི་སེམས་གསལ་སྟོང་ལས་མ་གཡོས་པར་ཁོ་ཐག་ཆོད་ནས་རྣམ་རྟོག་སྣ་ཚོགས་པ་སེམས་སུ་ངེས་པའི་སྤྱོད་པ་ཐོན་དགོས་ཤིང་།

You may not have found that the thought arose from a particular location in a particular way, that it dwells in a particular shape or form or that it departs to a particular place. Nevertheless, your concepts about whether thought and mind are different, whether they are related as inside and outside, or as the body and its limbs and so forth must be destroyed. You must experience that the various thoughts, in whatever form they arise, are an empty appearance and not a definable entity. You must recognize that they arise out of yourself and dissolve into yourself. Since mind is unconfined, you must become certain that it is mind that merely appears or is seen as being thoughts. You must resolve that thoughts and mind are indivisible.

Take the metaphor of a wave on water. The wave is nothing other than the water, and yet it is seen as a wave. Although it appears as a wave, it has never changed from being of the nature of water. In the same way, with the various types of thoughts, from the very moment they appear, they are nothing other than the aware emptiness of unidentifiable mind.

Moreover, since this mind is unconfined, it does appear as a variety of thoughts. Even though it appears as them, it has not changed from being the aware emptiness of the mind that is not a definable entity. You must settle this point decisively. You must gain the experience of certainty in the fact that the various types of thoughts are mind.

Similarly, give rise to a happy or a sad thought and investigate whether there is any difference in their identity.

དེ་བཞིན་ཏུ་སྐྱིད་པའི་རྟོག་པ་ཞིག་དང་སྡུག་པའི་རྟོག་པ་ཞིག་སྤྲོས་ལ་དེ་གཉིས་ཀྱི་ངོ་བོ་ལ་ཁྱད་ཅི་འདུག་བལྟ་བ་སོགས་རྒྱུབ་བསྒོལ་གྱི་རྟོག་པ་ཡང་ཐག་ཆོད་པར་བྱའོ།།

གཉིས་པ་ནི། ལུས་གནད་སོགས་སྔར་ལྟར་བྱས་ཏེ་སེམས་གསལ་སྟོང་གི་ངང་ནས་གཟུགས་སྣང་གང་ཡང་རུང་བ་ཞིག་རྣམ་པ་གསལ་ལམ་གྱིས་འཆར་དུ་བཅུག་ལ། དེའི་བྱུང་གནས་འགྲོ་གསུམ་གོང་བཞིན་བརྟག།

གཟུགས་སྣང་དང་སེམས་གཉིས་ཐ་དད་དུ་འདུག་གམ་གཅིག་ཏུ་འདུག། ཐ་དད་ན་ཕན་ཚུན་ནམ་ཕྱི་ནང་ངམ་སྟེང་འོག་ལྟ་བུར་འདུག་གམ།

དེ་ལྟར་འདུག་ན་རང་ཚུགས་ཐུབ་པའི་ངོ་བོ་སོ་སོར་གྲུབ་པ་འདུག་གམ་སེམས་དེར་སྣང་བ་ཙམ་དུ་འདུག།

སེམས་དེར་སྣང་བ་ཙམ་ལ་སེམས་གཅིག་ལས་མེད་པ་ཐ་དད་དུ་འགལ་བར་བརྟག། གཟུགས་སྣང་དང་སེམས་གཅིག་ན་སེམས་གཟུགས་སྣང་དུ་སོང་ནས་གཅིག་གམ་གཟུགས་སྣང་སེམས་སུ་སོང་ནས་གཅིག་ལ་སོགས་པ་བརྟག་ཏུ་བཅུག་ལ་ཉམས་བལྟ།

ལོག་ཤེས་འདུག་ན་གནོད་བྱེད་གཏོང་ཞིང་ཕྱོགས་བསྟན་ཏེ། གཟུགས་ཀྱི་སྣང་བ་གང་སྣང་སེམས་ཀྱི་སྣང་ཆ་ཙམ་དུ་ངེས་ནས་གཟུགས་ཀྱི་རྣམ་པ་སྣ་ཚོགས་པར་སྣང་ཡང་ངོ་བོ་ངོས་བཟུང་དུ་གྲུབ་པ་མེད་པ་སྣང་སྟོང་དུ་སྐྱོང་ཞིང་།

In this way, also become certain in regard to opposing types of thoughts.

Resolving That Perceptions Are Mind

Assume the physical posture as before and from within the state of aware and empty mind allow the appearance of any visual form to be vividly experienced. Investigate its arrival, remaining and departure, as above.

Now investigate the following points. Is the visual perception different from or identical to mind? If different, are they across from each other, one inside the other or one above the other? If that is the case, do they exist as separate entities that can stand alone?

Or is it merely an instance of the mind seen as a visual perception? In the case of it being only the mind that appears as such, there is nothing more than a single mind, and that contradicts them being different.

If the visual perception is identical with mind, are they identical in that it is mind that turns into the visual perception, or are they identical in that it is the visual perception that becomes mind? Investigate in this way to gain personal experience. If there is an incorrect understanding, it should be counteracted and a hint given.

In this way, no matter what visual perception you see, you must become certain that it is merely the mind's perceiving quality. No matter which of the various types of visual forms you see, you must personally experience that it has no definable identity but is a perceived emptiness. Since mind's expressive power is unconfined, you must

སེམས་ཀྱི་རྩལ་མ་འགགས་པས་གཟུགས་ལ་སོགས་པའི་རྣམ་པར་སྣང་བ་ཙམ་དུ་རིག་ནས།

གཟུགས་སྣང་ཕྱིར་མ་ལུས་སེམས་ནང་དུ་མ་ལུས་པར་སྣང་སེམས་དབྱེར་མེད་དུ་ཐག་ཆོད་དགོས་ལ།

དཔེ་དོན་གོང་དུ་བཤད་པ་ལྟར་རམ་རྨི་ལམ་ན་ཕྱི་རོལ་གྱི་གཟུགས་སྣ་ཚོགས་པ་ཤར་ཡང་རྨི་ལམ་གྱི་ཤེས་པ་ལས་མ་འདས་ཤིང་རྨི་ལམ་གྱི་གཟུགས་དང་རྨི་ལམ་གྱི་ཤེས་པ་དབྱེར་མེད་པ་ལྟ་བུའོ།།

གནས་སྐབས་སྤྱི་མཐུན་གྱི་ལས་ཀྱིས་སྣང་བའི་ཡུལ་རྐྱེན་གྱིས་སོ་སོ་སྣ་ཚོགས་པར་སྣང་བ་ནི།

དཔེར་ན་ཤེལ་དྭངས་པ་ཞིག་ཡུལ་རྐྱེན་སྔོན་པོ་སོགས་དང་འཕྲད་ན་སྔོན་པོ་སོགས་སུ་སྣང་ཙམ་ལས་ངོ་བོ་ཤེལ་དྭངས་པ་དེ་ཉིད་ལས་གཞན་དུ་མ་སོང་བ་ལྟར།

སྒོ་མ་འགག་པའི་སེམས་ལས་མ་དག་པར་དུ་ཡུལ་རྐྱེན་སྣ་ཚོགས་དང་འཕྲད་ན་སྣ་ཚོགས་སུ་སྣང་ཙམ་ལས་ངོ་བོ་སེམས་ལས་གཞན་དུ་མ་སོང་བར་ཐག་ཆོད་ནས་སྣང་བ་སྣ་ཚོགས་སེམས་སུ་ངེས་པའི་སྦྱོང་བ་ཐོན་དགོས།

recognize that it merely appears as visual form and so forth. Do not keep visual perception and mind separate as outside and inside; settle decisively that perceptions and mind are indivisible.

Just like the example and meaning explained above, or like the various visual forms that may appear external to be in a dream, although they are nothing other than the dreaming mind, so the dream-forms and the dreaming mind are indivisible.

❧

The myriad different types of things that are presently experienced, due to the incidence of objects appearing by the power of 'shared karma', are like the example of a clear mirror that is only perceived to be blue when meeting with the circumstance of a blue object and so forth. In fact, the mirror has not turned into anything other than its identity of being a clear mirror.

Likewise, as long as this unconfined mind has not been purified of karma, it appears in various ways when meeting with the circumstances of different types of objects. In fact, the mind has not turned into anything other than mind itself. Having resolved this, you must gain the experience of certainty in the fact that the various types of perceptions are mind.

In a similar fashion to that above, investigate the opposing perceptions of beautiful and ugly things. As exemplified by visual forms, also examine sounds, odors, flavors and textures, and make sure you gain certainty.

དེ་བཞིན་དུ་མཛོས་མི་མཛོས་སོགས་རྒྱབ་འགལ་གྱི་སྣང་བ་གོང་ལྟར་བརྟག། གཟུགས་ཀྱིས་མཚོན་ནས་སྒྲ་དྲི་རོ་རེག་བྱ་ལ་སོགས་པ་ཐམས་ཅད་བརྟགས་ནས་ངེས་པ་རྙེད་པར་བྱའོ།།

གསུམ་པ་ནི། ལུས་གནད་སྔར་ལྟར་བྱས་ལ་སེམས་གསལ་སྟོང་གི་ངང་དུ་ལྷན་ནེ་གནས་སུ་བཅུག་སྟེ་དེ་ལ་ཅེར་གྱིས་བལྟས་ནས་བརྟག།

ཡང་ལྷན་གནས་པའི་ངང་ནས་འགྱུ་བ་ཞིག་ཡེར་གྱིས་འགྱུར་བཅུག་སྟེ་དེ་ལ་བལྟས་ནས་བརྟག།

དེ་ནས་གནས་པ་དང་འགྱུ་བ་གཉིས་ཀྱི་བྱུང་གནས་འགྲོ་གསུམ་དང་ངོ་བོ་ངོས་བཟུང་གི་ཁྱད་པར་ཅི་འདུག་བརྟག།

ལྷན་གནས་པ་དང་ཡེར་ཤར་བའི་ཁྱད་པར་འདུག་ན། དེ་གཉིས་རང་ལ་བཟང་ངན་དང་སྟོང་མ་སྟོང་དང་ངོ་བོ་གྲུབ་མ་གྲུབ་དང་ངོས་བཟུང་ཡོད་མེད་ཀྱི་ཁྱད་པར་ཅི་འདུག་ལ་སོགས་པ་བརྟག། ཁྱད་པར་མེད་ན་གཅིག་ནས་ཁྱད་པར་མེད་དམ་ཐ་དད་ཀྱང་མཚུངས་ནས་ཁྱད་པར་མེད་བརྟག།

གཅིག་ན་ཐོག་མཐའ་བར་གསུམ་གང་དུ་གཅིག་བརྟག།

མཚུངས་ན་ཇི་ལྟར་མཚུངས་ལ་སོགས་པ་བརྟག་དཔྱད་བྱེད་དུ་བཅུག་ལ་ཉམས་བལྟ། ལོག་ཤེས་འདུག་ན་མཐའ་བཀག་ཅིང་ཕྱོགས་བསྟན་ལ་སླར་བརྟག་ཏུ་བཅུག།

Investigating the Calm and the Moving Mind

Maintain the same physical posture as mentioned before. Let your mind be serenely calm in the state of aware emptiness. Now, investigate by looking directly into it.

While in this state of serene calm allow a thought to vividly stir. Investigate it too by looking directly into it.

Next, investigate the two instances of calm and thought movement to see if there is any difference in their arrival, remaining and departure or in their definable identity.

If there is a difference between remaining calmly and an abrupt movement of thought, examine to see if their difference consists in being better or worse, empty or not empty, having or not having an identity, and between being or not being identifiable.

If there is no difference, investigate to see if their lack of disparity consists in being identical or in being similar while different.

If identical, investigate how they are identical at the beginning, middle and end. If similar, examine how they are similar. Investigate in this way to gain some experience.

In case an incorrect understanding is held, it should be stopped with a counter-argument, a hint should be given and the investigation resumed.

Turning away from the belief that these two — serene calm and abrupt thought movement — are of entirely different substances, you must experience that they are the same mind, the mind that is identical in being rootless and intangible, and in being an aware emptiness that is self-knowing and naturally pure.

ལྷན་ཅིར་གནས་པ་དང་ཡེར་གྱིས་འགྱུས་པ་གཉིས་རྒྱུད་ཐ་དད་དུ་འཛིན་པ་ལས་ལོག་སྟེ། གཉིས་ཀ་སེམས་ཉིད་གཅིག་པུ་རྩ་བྲལ་ངོས་བཟུང་མེད་པ་རང་རིག་རང་དག་གསལ་སྟོང་དུ་ངོ་བོ་གཅིག་པ་མྱོང་ནས།

དེ་གཉིས་གང་བྱུང་ཡང་དགག་སྒྲུབ་སྤང་བླང་མི་དགོས་པར་གནས་ན་གནས་ཐོག་འགྱུ་ན་འགྱུ་ཐོག་དེ་གསལ་སྟོང་རང་གྲོལ་དུ་ངེས་ཤེས་སྐྱེ་དགོས་པ་ཡིན་ནོ།།

བཞི་པ་ནི། སྔར་བཞིན་སེམས་གསལ་སྟོང་གི་ངང་ན་རྣམ་རྟོག་དང་སྣང་བ་སྣ་ཚོགས་ནི་སེམས་འདི་ཀ་མ་འགགས་པའི་རྩལ་སྣང་དུ་འདུག།

ད་ནི་སེམས་འདི་ཀའི་རང་བབས་འདི་ཅི་ལྟ་བུ་སྙམ་དུ་ཅེར་གྱིས་བལྟས་པ་ལ་འདིའི་རྒྱུ་གང་ལས་བྱུང་ཚུལ་ཇི་ལྟར་གནས་མཐར་ཇི་འདྲར་སོང་ལེགས་པར་བརྟག་ཏུ་བཅུག།

ལོག་ཤེས་འདུག་ན་མཐའ་དགག་ཅིང་ཕྱོགས་བསྟན་ལ་སླར་ཡང་བརྟག་ཏུ་བཅུག་ནས།

སེམས་དང་པོར་རྒྱུ་རྐྱེན་ལས་མ་བྱུང་གཞི་གང་ལས་ཀྱང་མ་སྐྱེས་པ་ཡེ་ནས་ཀྱི་རྩ་བྲལ།

འཕྲུལ་གྱི་དབྱིབས་རྣམ་འགྱུར་སོགས་གང་དུ་མི་གནས་ཤིང་ངོས་བཟུང་རྒྱུ་མེད་པ།

This being so, whichever of the two happens, there is no need to accept or reject, repress or encourage. Rather, you should become confident that this aware emptiness is naturally free — in the very stillness when calm and in the very arising when thoughts occur.

Resolving That All Experience Is Nonarising

While in the state of empty and aware mind, as before, the various types of thoughts and perceptions are the unconfined expressions of this very mind itself. Now, question this, "What is the natural state of this very mind?" Look directly and thoroughly investigate what caused it to arrive, how it remains and how it finally departs.

In case an incorrect understanding is held, it should be terminated with a counter-argument, a hint should be given and once more the investigation should be continued.

At the beginning, this mind was not produced from any causes or conditions, and did not arise from any basis, not in any way whatsoever; rather it is rootless since the beginning. Presently, it does not remain as any shape or form at all, but is unidentifiable. In the end, without being stopped by anyone, it is self-dissolving, self-clearing and self-liberated.

You must experience the actual mode of this mind: a self-knowing emptiness that from the very first cannot be pinpointed as arising, dwelling or ceasing. And, having done so, you must resolve that this mind, however it may presently appear, cannot be improved by anything good or

མཐར་སྲུས་ཀྱང་བཀག་པ་མེད་པར་རང་སངས་རང་དག་རང་གྲོལ་ལྟ་བུར་འདུག་པ་སྐྱོང་སྟེ།

གཏོད་མ་ནས་སྐྱེ་འགག་གནས་གསུམ་གྱི་ངོས་བཟུང་མེད་པར་རང་རིག་སྟོང་པ་ཉིད་ཡིན་པའི་ཡིན་ལུགས་ལྟར་གང་ཤར་གྱི་སེམས་ལ་བཟང་པོས་བརྒྱན་མི་ཚུགས་ངན་པས་སྦགས་མི་ཚུགས་པས་བཅོས་བསླད་དང་འཕྲོ་བསྟུན་མི་དགོས་པར་རང་དག་རང་རིག་རང་གྲོལ་ཉིད་དུ་ཐག་ཆོད་དགོས་སོ།།

དེ་ལྟར་ལྷག་མཐོང་གི་ལྟ་རྟོག་དང་གཞིག་འགྲེལ་ཐམས་ཅད་ལུས་གནད་དང་སེམས་གསལ་སྟོང་མཉམ་བཞག་གི་སྟེང་ནས་བརྟགས་ཤིང་དཔྱད་ན་ལྷག་མཐོང་གི་ཤེས་རབ་ཀྱིས་སྐྱོང་ལ། རྟོག་བཏགས་ཀྱི་བློ་ཁོ་ནས་དཔྱད་ན་དོན་སྤྱི་ཙམ་འཆར་སྲིད་ཀྱང་སྐྱོང་བ་མི་ཐོན་ནོ།།

འདི་ལ་ངེས་ཤེས་ཐག་ཆོད་པ་མ་སྐྱེས་ན་ངོ་སྤྲོད་ཀྱང་ཕྱིས་དེ་ལ་བློ་མི་ཁེལ་བར་གཞན་ལ་འཇུག་པའམ།

སྙིང་རུས་བསྐྱེད་ནས་བསྒོམས་ནའང་ཞི་གནས་ཙམ་པོ་བའི་སྟེང་དུ་འཁོར་ཏེ་དེའི་ཉམས་སྣང་ལ་ཞེན་པས་ལོ་མང་པོ་འབད་ཀྱང་བྱང་ཆུབ་ཏུ་བགྲོད་པའི་ས་མི་ཆོད་པ་ཡིན་ནོ།།

དེ་ལ་བློ་རབ་ཀྱིས་རྟོགས་པ་ཐོབ་པ་འབྲིང་གིས་སྐྱོང་བ་ཐོབ་པ་ཐ་མས་གོ་བ་བརྟན་པོ་ཐོབ་པ་དགོས་ཟེར་ཡང་གོ་བས་ཚུད་མི་འོང་ངོ་།

worsened by anything bad. As this is so, resolve that it is a self-clearing, self-knowing, self-liberated state that does not need to be fine-tuned or corrected.

When examining and observing in the meditation posture and within the composure of empty and aware mind, all these types of vipashyana investigations and considerations are experienced by means of vipashyana insight. On the other hand, if the examinations are made with an attitude of conceptual labeling, it is possible to gain a general idea, but not bring forth real experience.

Unless the meditators have resolved this with certainty, it is too early to receive the pointing-out instruction, since they will fail to trust it and pursue something else. Or, even if they practice with tenacity, they will linger in ordinary states of shamatha. Clinging to the meditative moods and states of shamatha will not effectively bring them to enlightenment even though they may strive for many years.

It is said that the person of the highest acumen must attain realization, the middling gain experience, and the lesser type must reach a stable understanding. It is, however, not enough to merely understand.

There are those who are good at explaining but lack personal experience and those who have the experience but cannot explain. The lama must, therefore, skillfully guide by counter-arguments and hints, and ask clever questions while pulling the wool over their eyes.[6]

Even when a sound experience has taken place, it is my opinion that the pointing-out instruction should definitely

འདི་དག་ལ་བཤད་མཁས་ཀྱང་སྒྲོང་བ་མ་ཐོན་པ་དང་སྒྲོང་ཡང་བཤད་མི་ཤེས་པ་ཡོང་བས་བླ་མས་མཐའ་གཙན་ཞིང་ཕྱོགས་སྟོན་པའི་སློ་ནས་ཁྲིད་མཁས་དང་མགོ་གཡོགས་ལ་འདྲི་མཁས་བྱ།

སྒྲོང་བ་དགའ་མོ་སྐྱེས་འདུག་ནའང་ཁ་ཡང་གིས་ངོ་སྤྲོད་བྱ་ཤོར་དུ་སོང་བ་ཡེ་མི་བྱ་བར་སོམ་མོ།།

རེ་ཞིག་སྒྲོང་དུ་བཙུག་གོ།།

ཁ་ཅིག་ལྷག་མཐོང་གི་ཁྲིད་དང་ངོ་སྤྲོད་སྤེལ་མར་བྱེད་པ་དང་ངོ་སྤྲོད་ཀྱི་སྐབས་སུ་བལྟ་ཉུལ་བྱེད་པ་སྣ་ཚོགས་སྣང་ཡང་།

འདི་དག་གི་སྐབས་སུ་དཔྱད་གཞིག་གིས་ཐག་བཅད་ལ་སྒྲོང་བ་བསྐྱེད་དེ་ངོ་སྤྲོད་ཀྱི་སྐབས་སུ་སྒྲོང་བ་ངོ་སྤྲད་ལ་སློམ་དུ་གཞུག་པ་དེ་ཀ་ལེགས་པ་ཡིན་ལ།

འདི་ཅི་ནས་ཀྱང་སྒྲོང་བ་སྐྱེ་མ་ཚུགས་ན་རེ་ཞིག་ཞི་གནས་དེ་ཉིད་གསལ་རིག་ཐོན་པ་སྐྱོང་དུ་བཙུག་ལ་ཅི་ཞིག་ན་ཁྲིད་པས་དོན་གྲུབ་ནས་སྒྲོང་བ་བརྟན་པ་འོང་ངོ་།

not be given too liberally. For a while the meditators should gain more experience.

❧

It appears that there are some who alternate guidance in vipashyana with the pointing-out instruction and some who employ investigations during the pointing-out instruction. Although there are a variety of such ways, in these contexts the best is simply to use investigation to resolve and bring forth personal experience. Thus, at the time of the pointing-out instruction the lama can point out what the experience is and launch the meditator upon training in it.

If, however, some personal experience is plainly not established, the meditator should, for a while, train in bringing forth the awake quality within the state of shamatha. This will, at a certain point, be achieved through proper guidance, after which a stable experience will take place.

གཉིས་པ་ངོ་སྤྲོད་པའི་རིམ་པ་ལ་གཉིས།

ལྷན་སྐྱེས་ངོ་སྤྲོད་པ་ལ་དངོས་དང་།

སྐྱོན་སེལ་ཞིང་སྒོམ་པ་ངོས་བཟུང་བའོ།།

དང་པོ་ལ་གསུམ།

སེམས་ཉིད་ལྷན་སྐྱེས་ངོ་སྤྲོད་པ།

རྣམ་རྟོག་ལྷན་སྐྱེས་ངོ་སྤྲོད་པ།

སྣང་བ་ལྷན་སྐྱེས་ངོ་སྤྲོད་པའོ།།

དང་པོ་ནི། ངོ་སྤྲོད་བྱེད་པའི་ཚེ་བླ་མ་དང་སློབ་མ་མིན་པར་གཞན་ཕག་ཏུ་རང་མི་བཞག་པར་སྒྲོན་ལུས་གནད་སྔར་ལྟར་བྱེད་དུ་བཅུག་སྟེ།

ཁྱོད་ཀྱིས་སེམས་མ་བཅོས་པར་རང་ལུགས་སུ་བཞག་པའི་དུས་ན་རྣམ་པར་རྟོག་པ་ཕྲ་རགས་ཐམས་ཅད་རང་སར་ཞི་ནས་སེམས་ཉིད་རང་ལུགས་སུ་གནས་པ་ཞིག་འདུག་གམ་མཉམ་པར་ཞོག་ལ་ལྟོས་དང་ཞེས་བལྟར་བཅུག།

དེ་ལ་ཞི་གནས་ཟེར་བ་ཡིན།

Steps of Pointing-Out Instruction

This has two parts:

The actual pointing-out of the innate
Eradicating faults and identifying the meditation practice

The Actual Pointing Out of the Innate

This has three aspects:

Pointing out innate mind-essence
Pointing out innate thinking
Pointing out innate perception

Pointing Out Innate Mind-Essence

First, when giving the pointing-out instruction, no one else should be present besides the master and disciple. If you prefer, assume the posture as before. Then the master says:

"Let your mind be as it naturally is without trying to correct it. Now, isn't it true that all your thoughts, both subtle and gross, subside in themselves? Rest evenly and look to see if this mind doesn't remain calm in its own natural state."

The master lets the disciple look.

"That's called shamatha."

དེའི་ངང་ནས་སྨུགས་པའམ་ལུང་མ་བསྟན་ནམ་ཕྱལ་བར་མ་སོང་བར་སེམས་ཀྱི་ངོ་བོ་དེ་འདི་འདྲ་ཞེས་ངག་ཏུ་སྨྲར་མ་རྩུགས་སེམས་ཀྱིས་བསམ་དུ་མེད་པ་ངོས་བཟུང་ཐམས་ཅད་དང་བྲལ་བ་གསལ་ལ་མ་འགགས་པ་རང་གིས་རང་རིག་པའི་ཤེས་པ་སེང་ངེ་བ་ལྟ་བུ།

སྐྱོང་རྒྱུ་མེད་པའི་སྐྱོང་རྒྱུ་འདྲ་བ་ཞིག་འདུག་གམ་མཉམ་བཞག་གི་ངང་ནས་ལྟོས་དང་ཞེས་བལྟར་བཅུག།

དེ་ལ་ལྷག་མཐོང་ཟེར་བ་ཡིན།

དེ་གཉིས་འདིར་བརྗོད་པ་སྔ་ཕྱི་ཡོད་ཀྱང་དོན་ལ་ཞི་གནས་དེ་དང་ལྷག་མཐོང་དེ་ཐ་དད་དུ་མེད་པར་ཞི་གནས་དེ་ཡང་ངོས་བཟུང་མེད་པའི་རང་རིག་རང་གསལ་གྱི་ལྷག་མཐོང་དེར་འདུག་གམ། ལྷག་མཐོང་དེ་ཡང་རང་ལུགས་སུ་གནས་ཤིང་རྣམ་རྟོག་གི་མཚན་མས་མ་གོས་པའི་ཞི་གནས་དེར་འདུག་གམ། མཉམ་བཞག་གི་ངང་ནས་ལྟོས་དང་ཞེས་བལྟར་བཅུག།

དེ་ལ་ཞི་ལྷག་ཟུང་འཇུག་ཟེར།

གཉིས་ཀ་སེམས་སྐད་ཅིག་མའི་ཐོག་ཏུ་ཚང་བ་ཡིན། འདི་སྐྱོང་ནས་ངོ་ཤེས་པ་ལ་སྒོམ་སྐྱེས་པ་ཟེར་བ་ཡིན། འདི་ནི་སངས་རྒྱས་ཀྱི་དགོངས་པ་སེམས་ཅན་གྱི་སེམས་ཉིད་སྐྱེ་མེད་ཆོས་སྐུ་གཤིས་ཀྱི་གནས་ལུགས་ལྷན་སྐྱེས་ཀྱི་སེམས་གཉུག་མའི་ཤེས་པ་ཕྱག་རྒྱ་ཆེན་པོ་སོགས་མིང་གི་རྣམ་གྲངས་མང་ཞིང་།

"During this state, do not become dull, absent-minded or apathetic. Is it not true that you cannot verbally formulate that the identity of this mind is such-and-such, nor can you mentally form a thought of it? Rather, isn't it a totally unidentifiable, aware, unconfined and lucid wakefulness that knows itself by itself?

"Within the state of evenness, look to see whether it isn't an experience without any 'thing' experienced."

The master then lets the disciple look.

"That's called vipashyana."

❧

"Here, these two are mentioned sequentially, but in actuality this kind of shamatha and vipashyana are not separate. Rather, look to see if this shamatha isn't the vipashyana that is an unidentifiable, self-knowing, natural awareness. Also look to see if this vipashyana isn't the shamatha of abiding in the natural state untainted by conceptual attributes. Rest evenly and look!"

The master lets the disciple look.

"That's called the unity of shamatha and vipashyana."

❧

"Both are contained within your present mind. Experiencing and recognizing this is called *the birth of meditation practice*.

"This is what is given many names, such as buddha-mind, mind-essence of sentient beings, nonarising dhar-

མདོ་རྒྱུད་བསྟན་བཅོས་མན་ངག་རྣམ་དག་ཐམས་ཅད་འདིའི་ཐོག་ཏུ་འབབ་ཅིང་གཞོལ་བ་ཡིན་ནོ།།

ཞེས་དང་སྒྲོ་ན་ཐོག་ཏུ་ཕོག་པའི་ལུང་འདྲེན་ཡང་བྱས་ལ་ངེས་ཤེས་བསྐྱེད།

གཞན་ནི་རེ་ཞིག་བཤད་པ་མང་ན་བློ་རྒྱུད་མགོ་འཁོར་སྲིད་པས་མི་དགོས་སོ།།

དོན་དྲིལ་བ་ལ་སེམས་རང་བབས་སུ་བཞག་པས་རྟོག་པ་རང་སར་གྲོལ་ནས་ངོས་བཟུང་མེད་པའི་རང་རིག་རང་གསལ་གྱི་སེམས་ལྷན་སྐྱེས་དེའི་ངང་དུ་རྩེ་གཅིག་ཏུ་ཞོག་ལ་མ་ཡེངས་པ་གྱིས།

ཐུན་མཚམས་ཀྱི་སྤྱོད་ལམ་རྣམས་སུ་ཡང་དེའི་དྲན་པ་མ་ཡེངས་པ་ཅི་ཐུབ་གྱིས་ལ་ཞག་འགར་འཇུར་ཐོན་པར་སྒོམ་པ་གལ་ཆེ།

དེ་མིན་ཐབས་སྣ་ཚོགས་ཀྱིས་བཙལ་བའི་སེམས་ངོ་མཐོང་བ་འདི་ཤོར་དོགས་ཡོད་ཅེས་གཟུན་ལ་ཞག་འགའ་སྒོམ་དུ་བཅུག།

གཉིས་པ་ནི། སྔར་བཞིན་མདུན་དུ་ལུས་གནད་བྱེད་དུ་བཅུག།

makaya, basic natural state, innate mind, original wakefulness, Mahamudra, and so forth. And this is what all the sutras and tantras, true treatises and instructions aim at and lead to."

❧

Having said this, if the master prefers, he can inspire further confidence by giving relevant quotations from the scriptures. Otherwise, it may not be necessary to say more than the following, since some people of lesser intelligence may get confused when the explanation is too long.

"The meaning in a nutshell is this: allow your mind to be as it naturally is, and let thoughts dissolve in themselves. This is your innate mind, which is an unidentifiable, self-knowing, natural awareness. Remain one-pointedly in its continuity and do not get distracted.

"During the daily activities between breaks as well, try to keep this kind of mindfulness undistractedly as much as you can.

"It is important to continue training persistently for a couple of days. Otherwise, there may be a danger of this seeing of mind-essence, which you have pursued through various means, slipping away."

The meditator should therefore train in focusing on that for a couple of days.

ཁྱོད་རང་སེམས་རང་ལུགས་སུ་བཞག་སྟེ་རྣམ་རྟོག་ཞི་ནས་ངོས་བཟུང་མེད་པའི་སེམས་གསལ་སྟོང་རྗེན་ནེ་གནས་དུས་ཀྱི་ངོ་བོ་ལ་མ་ཡེངས་པའི་ངང་ནས་ཅེར་གྱིས་ལྟོས།

ཡང་དགའ་སྐྱིད་ལྟ་བུའི་རྣམ་རྟོག་ངར་དང་བཅས་པ་ཞིག་འགྱུར་ཆུགས་ལ་དེ་ལམ་སྟེ་སྐྱེས་པ་དང་དེའི་ངོ་བོ་ལ་གསལ་སྟོང་གི་ངང་ནས་ཅེར་ལྟོས་ལ།

རྣམ་རྟོག་དེ་ཡང་ངོས་བཟུང་མེད་པའི་གསལ་སྟོང་དུ་རྗེན་ནེ་འདུག་གམ།

སེམས་ཉིད་ལྷན་སྐྱེས་ཀྱི་ངོ་བོ་དང་ཁྱད་མེད་པ་དེ་གར་འདུག་གམ་ལྟོས་དང་ཞིབ་དར་ཅིག་བལྟར་བཅུག

གསལ་སྟོང་དུ་འདུག་ཁྱད་མི་སྣང་ཟེར་ཡང་།

རྣམ་རྟོག་དེ་སངས་ནས་གསལ་སྟོང་དུ་འདུག་གམ་རྣམ་རྟོག་དེ་ཚུར་སྒོམ་ལ་བཞག་པས་གསལ་སྟོང་དུ་འདུག་གམ་རྣམ་རྟོག་ལམ་མེ་བ་དེ་ག་གསལ་སྟོང་དུ་འདུག་དྲིས་པས།

སྔ་མ་གཉིས་ལྟར་འདུག་ཟེར་ན་སྔར་སྒྲོ་འདོགས་མ་ཆོད་པ་ཡིན་པས་ཞག་འགའ་ཐག་བཅད་དུ་འཇུག

དང་པོ་གཉིས་མ་དགོས་པར་ཕྱི་མ་ལྟར་འདུག་པ་སྨྲོང་ན་རྣམ་རྟོག་གི་ངོ་བོ་མཐོང་བ་ཡིན་པས་ངོ་སྤྲོད་པ་ནི།

Pointing Out Innate Thinking

Second, the meditator should now assume the correct posture in front of (the master, and be told the following):

"Let your mind remain in its natural way. When thoughts have subsided, your mind is an intangible, aware emptiness. Be undistracted and look directly into the identity of this naked state!

"At this moment, allow a feisty thought, such as delight, to take form. The very moment it vividly occurs, look directly into its identity from within the state of aware emptiness.

"Now, is this thought the intangible and naked state of aware emptiness? Or is it absolutely no different from the identity of innate mind-essence itself? Look!"

Let the meditator look for a short while.

The meditator may say, "It is the aware emptiness. There seems to be no difference." If so, ask:

"Is it an aware emptiness after the thought has dissolved? Or, is it an aware emptiness by driving away the thought by meditation? Or, is the vividness of the thought itself an aware emptiness?"

If the meditator says it is like one of the first two cases, he has not cleared up the former uncertainties and should therefore be set to resolve this for a few days.

On the other hand, if he personally experiences it to be like the latter case, he has seen the identity of thought and

ཁྱོད་ཀྱིས་རྣམ་རྟོག་གི་ངོ་བོ་ལ་བལྟས་པས་རྣམ་རྟོག་སངས་མ་དགོས་ཚུར་སྒོམ་ལ་གཙུར་མ་དགོས་པར་རྣམ་རྟོག་ལམ་མེ་བ་དེ་ཀ་ངོས་བཟུང་མེད་པ་གསལ་སྟོང་དུ་རྗེན་ནེ་འདུག་པ་དེ་ལ་རྣམ་རྟོག་ལྷན་སྐྱེས་ཀྱི་རང་ངོ་མཐོང་བའམ་རྣམ་རྟོག་ཆོས་སྐུར་ཤར་བ་ཟེར།

 སྤྱིར་རྣམ་རྟོག་གི་ངོ་བོ་གཏན་ལ་ཕབ་དུས་དང་གནས་འགྱུའི་རྩ་བ་བཅད་དུས་ལྷར་ངོས་བཟུང་མེད་པའི་སེམས་རང་རིག་རང་གསལ་གཅིག་པུ་དེ་མིན་པ་མང་པོ་མེད། རྩུ་དང་རླབས་ཀྱི་དཔེ་ལྟ་བུ་ཡིན།

དེས་ན་གནས་པ་དང་འགྱུ་བ་ལ་ཁྱད་འདུག་གམ་རྟོག་པ་དང་མ་རྟོག་པ་ལ་ཁྱད་འདུག་གམ།

མི་རྟོག་པར་ལྷན་གནས་པ་ལ་བཟང་རྒྱུའམ་དགའ་རྒྱུ་དང་རྣམ་རྟོག་ཡེར་འཕྲོས་པ་ལ་ངན་རྒྱུའམ་མི་དགའ་བ་དགོས་པ་འདུག་གམ།

འདིའི་མཚངས་མ་རིག་ན་སྒོམ་གྱི་མུ་གེ་ཡོག་པ་ཡིན་པས་ད་ཕྱིན་ཆད་རྟོག་པ་མ་སྐྱེས་ནས་སྐྱེས་པའི་ངང་དུ་སྐྱོངས་ཆེད་དུ་སྐྱེད་མི་དགོས།

སྐྱེས་ན་སྐྱེས་པའི་ངང་དུ་སྐྱོངས་ཆེད་དུ་དགག་མི་དགོས་པས་གནས་འགྱུ་གཉིས་ལ་ཉེ་རིང་མ་བྱེད།

རྣམ་རྟོག་འདིས་རྣམ་རྟོག་ཐམས་ཅད་ལ་འགྲེ་བ་ཡིན།

འོན་ཀྱང་རེ་ཞིག་ལ་རྣམ་རྟོག་ཉིད་ལམ་དུ་ཁྱེར་ཞིང་རྣམ་རྟོག་མ་སྐྱེས་ནའང་ཆེད་དུ་སྤྲོས་ལ་དེའི་ངོ་བོ་སྐྱོངས།

can therefore be given the following pointing-out instruction:

"When you look into a thought's identity, without having to dissolve the thought and without having to force it out by meditation, the vividness of the thought is itself the indescribable and naked state of aware emptiness. We call this *seeing the natural face of innate thought* or *thought dawns as dharmakaya*.

"Previously, when you determined the thought's identity and when you investigated the calm and the moving mind, you found that there was nothing other than this intangible single mind that is a self-knowing, natural awareness. It is just like the analogy of water and waves.

"This being so, is there any difference between calm and movement?

"Is there any difference between thinking and not thinking?

"Is it better to be serenely calm? Do you need to be elated about it?

"Is it worse when a thought abruptly arises? Do you need to be unhappy about it?

"Unless you perceive this hidden deception, you will suffer the *meditation famine*.[7] So, from now on, when a thought does not arise you need not deliberately make one arise so as to train in the state of its arising, and when the thought does arise you need not deliberately prevent it, so as to train in the state of its nonarising. Thus, do not be biased toward calm or movement."

དེ་མིན་རྣམ་རྟོག་གི་ངོ་བོ་མཐོང་བ་ཤོར་དོགས་ཡོད་པས་འབྱུངས་ལ་སྐྱོངས་ཞེས་གཙུན་ལ་ཞག་འགའ་སྒོམ་དུ་བཅུག།

སྤྲོ་ན་ལུང་འདྲེན་ཡང་བྱས་ལ་ངེས་ཤེས་བསྐྱེད་དོ།།

གསུམ་པ་ནི། སྔར་བཞིན་ལུས་གནད་དང་ལྟ་སྟངས་སོགས་ངོ་བོའི་མཉམ་བཞག་གི་ངང་ནས་རིའམ་ཁང་ཁྱིམ་ལྟ་བུའི་གཟུགས་ཀྱི་སྣང་བ་བཀྲ་ལམ་གྱིས་འཆར་དུ་བཅུག་ལ།

ཤར་བ་དེ་ལ་ཅེར་བལྟས་པའི་ཚེ་སྣང་བ་ངོས་བཟུང་མེད་པར་གསལ་སྟོང་དུ་འདུག་གམ།

སེམས་ཉིད་ཀྱི་ངོ་བོ་གསལ་སྟོང་དུ་འདུག།

དེ་གཉིས་ཁྱད་ཅི་འདུག་རེ་ཞིག་ལྟོས་དང་ཞེས་བལྟར་བཅུག།

ཁྱད་མེད་པར་ངོས་བཟུང་མེད་པའི་གསལ་སྟོང་དུ་འདུག་ཟེར་ཡང་།

སྣང་བ་ཤར་བའི་རྣམ་པ་དེ་འགགས་ནས་གསལ་སྟོང་དུ་དུག་གམ།

རྣམ་པ་དེ་གསལ་སྟོང་དུ་བསྒོམས་པས་གསལ་སྟོང་དུ་འདུག་གམ།

རྣམ་པ་སྣང་བ་དེ་ཀ་གསལ་སྟོང་དུ་འདུག་དྲིས་པས་སྔས་མ་གཉིས་ལྟར་ཟེར་ན་སྔར་གདར་ཤ་མ་ཆོད་པ་ཡིན་པས་སླར་སྒོམ་དུ་བཅུག་ལ་ཐག་བཅད།

The principle for this thought can be applied to all thoughts. However, the meditator should train for a while in simply making use of thoughts, so when no thoughts arise, conjure one up on purpose and sustain its essence. Otherwise, there is a danger of losing sight of the identity of thoughts.

The meditator should, therefore, be instructed to continue practicing diligently for several days. If it is preferable, bring in some quotations to instill certainty.

Pointing Out Innate Perception

Third, the physical posture and so forth should be kept just as before. Then ask:

"While in the composure of the natural state, allow a visual perception, such as that of a mountain or a house, to be vividly experienced. When looking directly at the experience, is this perception itself an intangible aware emptiness? Or, is it the aware and empty nature of mind? Look for a while to see what the difference between them is."

Let the meditator look. He may say, "There is no difference. It is an intangible, aware emptiness." If so, then ask:

"Is it an aware emptiness after the perceived image has disappeared? Or, is the image an aware emptiness by means of cultivating the aware emptiness? Or, is the perceived image itself an aware emptiness?"

གཟུགས་ཀྱི་རྣམ་པ་ལམ་སྣང་བ་དེ་ཀ་སྣང་ཆ་མ་འགགས་པར་སྣང་ཙམ་ལས་ངོས་བཟུང་མེད་པར་གསལ་སྟོང་དུ་འདུག་པ་མྱོང་ན།

ངོ་སྤྲོད་པ་ནི། ཁྱོད་ཀྱིས་རི་དང་ཁང་ཁྱིམ་ལྟ་བུའི་སྣང་བ་བཀྲ་ལམ་གྱིས་ཤར་བའི་ཚེ་ཇི་ལྟར་སྣང་བའི་སྣང་ཆ་དེ་ཉིད་ཡལ་བའམ་བཀག་མ་དགོས་པར་སྣང་བ་དེ་ཉིད་སྣང་བཞིན་དུ་ངོས་བཟུང་མེད་པ་གསལ་སྟོང་དུ་འདུག་པ་དེ་སྣང་བའི་ངོ་བོ་མཐོང་བ་ཡིན།

སྔར་སྣང་བའི་ངོ་བོ་བལྟ་དུས་དང་སྣང་བ་སེམས་སུ་ཐག་བཅད་དུས་སྒྲོ་འདོགས་བཅད་པ་ལྟར།

སྣང་བ་ཕྱི་ན་མེད་སེམས་ཉིད་ནང་ན་མེད་སེམས་གསལ་སྟོང་དེ་ཉིད་སྣང་བར་ཤར་བ་མ་གཏོགས་གཞན་མེད།

རྨི་ལམ་གྱི་ཡུལ་དང་རྨི་ལམ་གྱི་ཤེས་པའི་དཔེ་ལྟ་བུ་ཡིན།

སྣང་བ་ཤར་ཙམ་ཉིད་ནས་ངོས་བཟུང་མེད་པའི་སྣང་སྟོང་རང་གྲོལ་ཉིད་ཡིན། སྣང་ལ་ངོས་བཟུང་མེད་པའི་སྣང་སྟོང་དུ་རྗེན་ནེ་བ་འདི་ལ་སྣང་བ་ལྷན་སྐྱེས་རང་ངོ་མཐོང་བའམ་སྣང་བ་ཆོས་སྐུར་ཤར་བ་ཟེར།

དེས་ན་སྟོང་པ་བཟང་རྒྱུ་མེད་སྣང་བ་ངན་རྒྱུ་མེད་སྣང་སྟོང་ཐ་དད་དུ་མེད་པས། སྣང་ན་སྣང་ཐོག་དུ་སྐྱོངས་ཆེད་དུ་སྣང་ཆ་མ་བཀག།

If the answer comes that it is one of the first two cases, the meditator has not thoroughly investigated the above and should therefore once more be sent to meditate and resolve this.

If he does experience that the vividly perceived visual image itself — unidentifiable in any way other than as a mere presence of unconfined perception — is an aware emptiness, the master should then give this pointing-out instruction:

"When you vividly perceive a mountain or a house, no matter how this perception appears, it does not need to disappear or be stopped. Rather, while this perception is experienced, it is itself an intangible, empty awareness. This is called *seeing the identity of perception*.

"Previously you cleared up uncertainties when you looked into the identity of a perception and resolved that perceptions are mind. Accordingly, the perception is not outside and the mind is not inside. It is merely, and nothing other than, this empty and aware mind that appears as a perception. It is exactly like the example of a dream-object and the dreaming mind.

"From the very moment a perception occurs, it is a naturally freed and intangible perceiving emptiness. This perceiving yet intangible and naked state of empty perception is called *seeing the natural face of innate perception* or *perception dawning as dharmakaya*.

"This being so, 'empty' isn't something better and 'perceiving' isn't something worse, and perceiving and being

སྟོང་ན་སྟོང་ཐོག་ཏུ་སྐྱོངས་ཆེད་དུ་སྟོང་ཆ་མ་བསྒྲུབ་པར་གང་ཤར་སྒོམ་དུ་ཁྱེར།

སྤང་བླང་དང་བཅས་བཅོས་བྱ་མི་དགོས་ཉམས་ལེན་གྱི་དྲན་པས་སྐྱོབ་ན་སྣང་སྲིད་ཐམས་ཅད་ཆོས་ཀྱི་སྐུ་ཕྱག་རྒྱ་ཆེན་པོ་ཡིན་པས་ད་ཕྱིན་ཆད་སྣང་སྟོང་ལ་དགག་སྒྲུབ་དང་ཉེ་རིང་མ་བྱེད་པར་སྐྱོངས།

འོན་ཀྱང་རེ་ཞིག་སྣང་བའི་འཆར་སྒོ་མི་འདྲ་བ་སྣ་ཚོགས་འཆར་དུ་བཅུག་ལ་སྣང་ལ་ངོས་བཟུང་མེད་པའི་ངོ་བོ་སྐྱོང་བ་ལ་མ་ཡེངས་པ་གལ་ཆེ། ཞེས་ཞག་འགའ་སྒོམ་དུ་བཅུག་ཅིང་སྤྲོ་ན་ལུང་འདྲེན་ཡང་བྱས་ལ་ངེས་ཤེས་བསྐྱེད་དོ།

༈ གཉིས་པ་སྒྲོན་སེལ་ཞིང་སྒོམ་པ་ངོས་བཟུང་བ་ལ་གཉིས།

ནོར་དང་སྒོམ་སྒྲོན་བཤད་པ་དང་། སྒོམ་སྒྲོན་མེད་བསྟན་པའོ།།

དང་པོ་ནི། དྭགས་པོ་བཀའ་བརྒྱུད་ལ་སྒོམ་ཕྱག་རྒྱ་ཆེན་པོ་ཞེས་ཉེ་ནླ་ལྟར་གྲགས་ཀྱང་། སོ་སོའི་གོ་ལུགས་ཀྱི་ཁྱད་པར་ལ་བརྟེན་ནས་བློའི་འཛིན་སྟངས་མི་འདྲ་བ་སྣ་ཚོགས་འོང་བར་སྣང་བས། གཞན་དག་ལ་དགག་པ་བྱ་བ་མིན་ཀྱང་རང་ལ་ཡིད་གཏོད་པ་དག་ལ་གོ་བ་བསྐྱེད་པའི་ཕྱིར་ཙུང་ཟད་བརྗོད་པར་བྱ་སྟེ།

empty are not separate entities. So, you can continue training in whatever is experienced. When perceiving, in order to deliberately train in perception, there is no need to arrest it. When empty, in order to deliberately train in emptiness, you do not need to produce it.

"Whenever you recall the mindful presence of practice, all of appearance and existence is the Mahamudra of dharmakaya, without the need to adjust, accept or reject. And so, from now on, continue the training without being biased toward perception or emptiness by repressing or encouraging either of them.

"Nevertheless, for a while allow various kinds of perceptions to take place. While perceiving it is essential to be undistracted from sustaining the unidentifiable essence."

Thus, let the meditator train for several days. If it is preferred, bring in some quotations to instill certainty.

Eradicating Faults and Identifying the Meditation Practice

This has two parts:
Describing mistakes and faulty meditation
Explaining flawless meditation practice

Describing Mistakes and Faulty Meditation

It is renowned as far as the sun and moon that in the Dakpo Kagyü tradition the meditation practice is Mahamudra. Apparently, there are a variety of notions of Mahamudra due to individual ways of comprehension. I

དེ་ཡང་སེམས་ཀྱི་གནས་ཆ་ཁོ་ན་གཙོ་བོར་བཟུང་ནས་སེམས་གནས་མཚོ་ལ་དར་ཆགས་པ་ལྟར་གྱུར་ཏེ་ཚོགས་དྲུག་གི་སྣང་བ་ཕྲ་རགས་འགགས་པའམ། མ་འགགས་ཀྱང་མི་གསལ་བ་ཞལ་པོ་ལྟ་བུར་སོང་བ་ལ་སྒོམ་དུ་བཟུང་ན། སྔ་མ་ནི་ཤིན་ཏུ་སྐྱོན་ཆེ་ལ་ཕྱི་མའང་ལྷེམ་པོ་ཞེས་བྱ་བ་སྐྱོན་ཅན་ཡིན་ནོ།།

ཡང་སྣང་བ་གསལ་མི་གསལ་གྱི་ཚོར་བ་མེད་པའི་དྲན་མེད་དུ་འདུག་པ་ལ་སྒོམ་དུ་བཟུང་ན་ལུང་མ་བསྟན་ན་ཡེངས་པ་སྟེ་འདི་ཡིན་མེད་དོ།།

ཡང་ན་རྣམ་རྟོག་སྔ་མ་འགགས་ཕྱི་མ་མ་སྐྱེས་པའི་བར་གྱི་ཤེས་པ་ཧད་པོ་ལ་སྒོམ་དུ་བཟུང་ན། དེ་ནི་ལྷག་མཐོང་གིས་མ་ཟིན་པས་སྐྱོན་ཆེ་ལ་ཟིན་ཡང་ཕྱུག་ཆེན་སྐྱོང་བ་དེ་ལས་མ་གཡོས་པར་འདོད་དགོས་པས་སྒོམ་གྱི་སྨུ་གི་འབྱུང་ངོ་།

ཡང་སེམས་བདེ་ལྷམ་མེ་གནས་པ་ཙམ་ལ་སྒོམ་དུ་ངོས་བཟུང་ན། དེ་ཡང་ལྷག་མཐོང་གིས་མ་ཟིན་འདུག་གམ་སྒོམ་མིན་ལ་ཟིན་ཡང་འཆར་སྒོ་ཐམས་ཅད་དགག་དགོས་ཤིང་མ་བཀག་ཀྱང་དཀར་ལྷང་བས་ཅུང་ཟད་མིན་ནོ།། ཡང་དུས་གསུམ་གྱི་རྟོག་པ་གང་ཡང་ཡིད་ལ་མི་བྱེད་པར་སྟོང་སང་ངེ་བ་ལ་སྒོམ་དུ་བཟུང་ན། དེ་ཡང་ལྷག་མཐོང་གིས་མ་ཟིན་ཞིང་སྣང་ཆ་བཀག་པའི་སྐྱོན་ཆེན་པོ་ཡིན་ལ་ཟིན་ཡང་འཆར་སྒོ་དང་སྣང་ཆ་མི་འདོད་པས་ཅུང་ཟད་མིན་ནོ།།

am not about to disprove others. I will, however, explain a little to encourage understanding in those who rely on me.

Specifically, when people place exclusive emphasis on mental calm, their calm mind becomes like a lake frozen over with ice, so that all gross and subtle perceptions of the six senses cease. Or, even if not ceasing, they become unclear and hazy. Believing this to be the meditation state, the former incidence is a grave fault, while the latter is the shortcoming known as the *inert state*.

There are also some who regard the meditation state as remaining in a mindless way that doesn't notice what is or what isn't. This is to be lost in oblivion with no idea about what's happening.

Some people take meditation to be a vacant state of mind in which the former thought has ceased and the following thought has not yet arisen.

These ways are not embraced by vipashyana and so are grave faults. Even when embracing such states with vipashyana, these people feel they have to remain unmoved from this *maintaining of Mahamudra*. Thus, it becomes a meditation famine.

Furthermore, some identify the meditation state as merely remaining in a state full of bliss. If so, they have not embraced it with vipashyana. Or, even if it is, they feel they have to block off all perceptual experiences. Even when not blocking, to regard perceptions as opponents is still not correct.

If a state of being utterly empty, free from keeping any thought of the three times in mind, is regarded as the

ཡང་གང་སྣང་ཅི་ཤར་ཅི་ཤར་ཐམས་ཅད་ལ་བདེན་མེད་ཀྱི་འཛིན་སྟངས་དང་མ་བྲལ་བར་སྐྱོང་བ་ལ་སྒོམ་དུ་བཟུང་ན། དངོས་མེད་དུ་འཛིན་པ་ཞེས་སྐྱོན་ཅན་ནོ།།

ཡང་དྲན་པ་མེད་པར་སྣང་བ་མཐའ་དག་ལ་དགག་སྒྲུབ་མི་བྱེ་བ་སྒོམ་དུ་བཟུང་ན། བཏང་སྙོམས་སུ་གནས་པ་སྟེ་གྱི་ན་ཙམ་མོ།།

འདི་རྣམས་ནི་ཕྱག་ཆེན་གྱི་སྒོམ་དུ་བདག་གིས་མ་མཐོང་ལ་སོ་སོའི་ལས་གསོག་ཚུལ་རེ་ཡང་ཡོད་དོ།།

ཡང་སེམས་གསལ་སིང་ངེ་བ་ལ་མི་རྟོག་པ་ཁོ་ན་སྒོམ་དུ་བཟུང་ན་རྟོག་པ་རང་སར་ཞི་ནས་རིག་པ་གསལ་ལ་ངོས་བཟུང་མེད་པ་སྒོམ་ཡིན་དུ་ཆུག་ཀྱང་མི་རྟོག་པ་ཅི་ནས་ཀྱང་དགོས་པར་འདོད་སྣང་བས་ཕྱོགས་རེ་བའོ།།

དེ་བཞིན་དུ་རྣམ་རྟོག་འཕྲོས་པའི་ཚེ་དེའི་འཕྲོ་བཅད་ནས་གསལ་ལ་མི་རྟོག་པར་འཛིན་དགོས་པའང་ཕྱོགས་རེ་སྟེ། གཉིས་ཀ་འགྱུ་བ་དང་སྣང་ཆ་གཏན་ལ་མ་ཕེབས་པའོ།།

ཡང་དྲན་རིག་ཧུར་རེ་བྱས་ནས་སེམས་གསལ་སྟོང་ཧྲིག་གེ་བ་ཁོ་ན་སྒོམ་དུ་བཟུང་ན།

དེ་ཉིད་སྒོམ་ཡིན་ཡང་དྲན་པ་ནྲབས་ཆེ་བའི་རང་བབས་ལྷུག་པར་མི་འདོད་པར་སྣང་བས་ལྷོད་ཆ་མ་རྙེད་པར་ཧ་ཅང་སྒྲིམ་པའི་ཕྱོགས་རེ་བའོ།།

meditation state, that too is not embraced by vipashyana and has the grave fault of blocking off perceptual experience. Even when embraced, it is still not correct since there is a dislike for experience and perception.

Or, if the meditation is regarded as constantly keeping the conceptual stance that all perceptions — whatever appears and is experienced — are insubstantial, this *clinging to inconcreteness* is a grave fault.

Moreover, if the meditation is regarded as absent-mindedly refraining from accepting or rejecting the entirety of perceptual experience, that is *indifferent calm* and is simply an ordinary state.

I do not see any of these stances as being the training in Mahamudra, but they do exist as various ways certain individuals create karma.

Again, a state of mind that is lucid and thoughtfree may exclusively be regarded as the meditation. The lucid and indescribable awareness, after a thought has subsided, is indeed the meditation training. However, if you feel you must be thoughtfree, it is still imperfect.

Similarly, when a thought stirs it is also imperfect to feel that you have to interrupt it and then remain lucid and thoughtfree.

Both of these are cases of not yet having established thought movement and perception.

Moreover, a wide-awake state of empty and aware mind after making yourself intensely mindful, may be regarded as the meditation. Even though this indeed is the meditation practice, it is still imperfect in the sense of disliking a

དེས་བསྒོམ་མིན་མིན་པ་འཆུགས་པ་ནི་ཤིན་ཏུ་གལ་ཆེ་ལ། སྒོམ་ཕྱོགས་རེ་བ་ལ་ཡར་འཕེལ་དུ་འགྲོ་བའི་ཡོན་ཏན་ཡོད་ཀྱང་།

སྐྱོང་མ་བདེ་ནས་སྒོམ་དང་སྣ་སྲུན་དོགས་ཡོད་པས་སྣང་ཐོག་སྟོང་ཐོག་གནས་ཐོག་འགྲུ་ཐོག་ཐམས་ཅད་དུ་གྲིམས་ལྷོད་སྣ་ཚོགས་པའི་སྒོ་ནས་གདར་ཤ་ཆོད་ཅིང་ངོ་འཕྲོད་པ་སྐྱོང་བདེ་བ་ཞིག་དགོས་པ་ཡིན་ནོ།།

གཉིས་པ་ནི། ཐ་མལ་གྱི་ཤེས་པ་མ་ཡེངས་པ་ལ་སྒོམ་ཞེས་བྱ་བ་ལས།

ཐ་མལ་གྱི་ཤེས་པ་ནི་སེམས་ཀྱི་རང་བབས་ཅི་འདུག་དེ་ཀ་ཡིན་ཏེ། དེ་ལ་སྤང་བླང་དང་དགག་སྒྲུབ་ཀྱི་བཅས་བཅོས་བྱས་ན་ཐ་མལ་གྱི་ཤེས་པར་མི་འགྲོའོ།།

དེས་ན་སེམས་ཀྱི་རང་བབས་ཅི་འདུག་ཅི་སྣང་ཅི་ཤར་དེ་རང་རིག་གི་དྲན་པས་མ་ཡེངས་པར་སྐྱོང་བ་ལ་སྒོམ་སྐྱོང་བ་ཞེས་མིང་ཙམ་འདོགས་ཀྱི།

བློས་བཅོས་ནས་སྒོམ་རྒྱུ་རྡུལ་ཙམ་ཡང་མེད་དོ།།

དེ་ལ་སྒོམ་རྒྱུ་རྡུལ་ཙམ་མེད་པ་ལ་ཡེངས་སུ་སྐད་ཅིག་ཙམ་ཡང་མེད་ཟེར་བ་དང་།

ཐ་མལ་ཤེས་པ་ཡེངས་མེད་འདི་ཞེས་པའང་མ་ཡེངས་པར་སེམས་རང་བབས་སྐྱོང་བ་ལ་ཟེར་རོ།།

natural, free and wide-open presence of mind and, instead, preferring to focus excessively in an unrelaxed way.

It is, therefore, extremely important not to be confused about the flawed ways of meditation practice.

The imperfect ways of training still have the possibility of progress, but they are awkward to sustain and so involve the risk of wearying of practice. Through various ways of focusing and relaxing in all instances — perceiving or being empty, thinking or being calm — you must thoroughly investigate and recognize, so as to find a comfortable way to sustain it.

Explaining Flawless Meditation Practice

Second, meditation practice is known as *undistracted ordinary mind*. *Ordinary mind* simply means your mind's natural state. When you try to correct it by judging, accepting or rejecting, it will no longer be your ordinary mind.

Therefore, undistractedly maintain the natural state of your mind with a naturally aware presence, no matter how it is or what is perceived or felt. That is simply called 'meditating'.[8] Other than that, there isn't even as much as a hair-tip to adjust mentally by meditating.

It is explained in this way: "While there isn't even as much as an atom to cultivate by meditating, you shouldn't be distracted for even as long as an instant." Phrased in another way, *undistracted ordinary mind* means to keep the way your mind naturally is without being distracted.

དེས་ན་རང་རིག་གི་དྲན་པ་མ་ཡེངས་ན་སེམས་སྟོང་སང་ངེ་བའམ་བདེ་ལམ་མེ་བར་གནས་པའམ།

རྣམ་རྟོག་འཚུབ་ཟིང་ངེ་འཁྲོ་བའམ་སྣང་བ་སྣ་ཚོགས་བཀྲ་ལམ་གྱིས་འཆར་ཡང་སྒོམ་ཡིན་པས་གནས་ལུགས་ཀྱི་རྒྱལ་ལ་ཟློ་འཕྲིག་མི་བྱ་བར་ལྷུག་པར་སྐྱོང་བ་ཡིན་གྱི་རྟོག་པ་འཁྲོ་བ་དང་སྣང་བ་བཀུག་པའམ་བཀག་ནས་མི་རྟོག་པར་འཛོག་པ་དོན་མིན་ནོ།།

དེའི་རྒྱུ་མཚན་ཡང་སྔར་སྒྲོ་འདོགས་བཅད་ཅིང་ངོ་སྤྲོད་པ་ལྟར་སེམས་ཉིད་ཀྱི་ངོ་བོ་དང་རྣམ་རྟོག་དང་སྣང་བའི་འཆར་སྒོ་སོགས་ཐ་དད་པ་མང་པོ་མེད་པར་སེམས་ཉིད་གཅིག་པུ་མ་འགགས་པའི་རྩལ་རྒྱ་མཚོ་ཉིད་རླབས་སུ་ཤར་བ་ལྟ་བུ་ཡིན་པས་སེམས་ཀྱི་རང་བབས་ཅི་ཤར་དེ་ལ་བཟང་ངན་མེད་དོ།།

དེས་ན་སེམས་གནས་ན་གནས་ཐོག་འགྱུ་ན་འགྱུ་ཐོག་སྣང་ན་སྣང་ཐོག་དེ་དྲན་པས་སྐྱོང་བ་ཡིན་ཏེ། གནས་ན་ཆེད་དུ་མི་སྤྲོ་འགྱུ་ན་མི་དགག་པར་གསལ་སང་ངེ་བའམ། སྟོང་ཆམ་མེ་བའམ་བདེ་ལྷམ་མེ་བའམ་འཚུབ་ཟིང་བ་ཅི་འདུག་ནའང་མ་ཡེངས་པ་ལས་བསྒྱུར་དགོད་བཅས་བཅོས་བྱ་མི་དགོས་སོ།།

མདོར་ན་རང་རིག་གི་དྲན་པ་དང་ལྡན་ན་ཐམས་ཅད་སྒོམ་ཡིན་ལ་ཡེངས་ན་གང་ཡང་སྒོམ་མིན་པས་རེ་ཞིག་ལ་དྲན་པ་རྗེས་སུ་བྱ་ཞིང་།

This being so, as long as your naturally aware mindful presence has not wandered off, it is still the meditation training, whether your state of mind is utterly empty, remains serenely blissful, whether thoughts flow in a rush or manifold perceptions appear vividly. Therefore, you do not need to entertain doubts about these expressions of the natural state. Rather than maintaining a sense of natural ease, there is no point in trying to arrest or block off the flow of thought or perception for the sake of remaining thoughtfree.

The reason is this: just like before, when you cleared up uncertainties and during the pointing-out instruction, various entities such as mind-essence, thought, perceptual experience and so forth do not exist. Rather, they are the unconfined expressions of this single mind, just like the ocean itself is what is seen as waves. Therefore, this natural flow of mind does not differ in quality, no matter how it appears.

This being so, you should sustain presence of mind in stillness when calm, in thinking when thoughts occur and in perceiving when perceptions take place. Do not deliberately try to think when still or prevent a thought when it occurs. No matter what your state may be — lucidly clear, totally empty, suffused with bliss or completely restless — simply remain undistracted. You do not need to modify or correct anything.

In short, everything is meditation training when you have naturally aware presence of mind and nothing is

ཅེ་ཞིག་ན་དྲན་པ་དང་སེམས་ཀྱི་ངོ་བོ་ཐ་མི་དད་པས་ཐམས་ཅད་དྲན་པའི་རང་བཞིན་དུ་གྱུར་ནས་བདེ་བ་ཞིག་འོང་ངོ་།

འོ་ན་ཁྲིད་རིམ་ལྟར་མི་དགོས་པར་དང་པོ་ཉིད་ནས་སེམས་ཅེ་ཤར་དྲན་པས་བཟུང་བས་ཆོག་གམ་སྙམ་ན་ཅིག་ཆར་བའི་ལས་ཅན་ཁ་ཅིག་ཙམ་དེ་ལྟ་བུས་ཆོག་པ་སྲིད་ཀྱང་།

གཞན་དུ་ཁྲིད་རིམ་ལྟར་འཁྲིད་པར་སྣང་སེམས་ཀྱི་རྩ་བ་སྒྲོ་འདོགས་མི་ཆོད་ཅིང་།

ངོ་བོ་མཐོང་བའི་སྙིང་བ་དང་བཅས་པའི་ངེས་ཤེས་མི་འབྱུང་བས་དྲན་པ་གཞན་ཡོད་ཀྱང་རང་རིག་གི་དྲན་པ་མེད་པས་མི་འོང་ངོ་།

དེས་ན་ཐ་མལ་གྱི་སེམས། མ་བཅོས་པ་གཉུག་མའི་སེམས་ཞེས་པའི་ཚིག་དོན་ཡང་འདིར་གནས་ལ་ལྟ་བ་རྣམ་དག་སྟོན་པའི་མདོ་རྒྱུད་དང་རྒྱ་བོད་ཀྱི་གྲུབ་ཆེན་རྣམས་ཀྱི་གསུང་རྣམས་ཀྱང་འདིར་གཞོལ་བ་ཡིན་ནོ།

meditation when you are distracted. Therefore, understand the great importance of maintaining this mindfulness.

At some point, when mindfulness and your mind are no longer different entities, everything turns into the nature of mindful presence and it is 'smooth sailing' from then on.[9]

You may now wonder, "Well, wouldn't it be enough simply to embrace whatever is experienced with mindfulness from the very first without having to follow gradual steps of guidance?" Yes, it might be enough for a few rare karmically destined people of the instantaneous type. For others, unless they follow the gradual steps of guidance to investigate and clear up uncertainties about perceptions and mind, they will not gain the certainty that accompanies the experience of seeing their essence. One may have other types of mindfulness, but these will not suffice unless it is the naturally aware mindful presence.

Consequently, the pivotal point here hinges on the words and meaning of *ordinary mind* and *uncontrived natural mind*. All the sutras, tantras and teachings of the siddhas of India and Tibet that express the true view lead to this point as well.

༄ གསུམ་པ་རྗེས་ཉམས་ལེན་སྐྱོང་ཚུལ་ལ་དྲུག།

སྤྱིར་སྐྱོང་དགོས་ཚུལ།

ཁྱད་པར་མཉམ་རྗེས་མི་བཅད་སྒོམ་སྐྱོང་ཚུལ།

གེགས་ཤོར་ས་དང་གོལ་ས་བཅད་པ།

སྐྱེ་མེད་དུ་ལ་བཟླས་ཏེ་བོགས་དབྱུང་བ།

ལམ་ཁྱེར་སྤྱོད་པའི་སྒོ་ནས་རྩལ་སྦྱོང་བ།

རྟོགས་པ་འཆར་ཚུལ་བོགས་འདོན་དང་བཅས་པའོ།།

དང་པོ་ནི། སྒོམ་སྐྱེས་པས་མི་ཆོག་ལེགས་པར་སྐྱོང་དགོས་ཏེ། སྒོམ་སྐྱེས་ནས་མ་བསྐྱངས་པར་ཐ་མལ་དུ་ལུས་པའམ་དམིགས་བཅས་ཀྱི་བསགས་སྦྱང་གཞན་ལ་འབད་པ་ནི་རྒྱལ་པོས་འབངས་ཀྱི་བྱ་བ་བྱེད་པའམ་སེང་གེ་ཁྱིའི་ཟླ་ལ་སོང་བ་ལྟར་དོན་ལས་ཡོག་པའོ།།

དེ་ལ་ཞེན་ལོག་སྒོམ་གྱི་རྐང་པའམ། བདག་པོ་ལྟ་བུ་ཡིན་པས་འཁོར་བའི་སྡུག་བསྔལ་བསམ། ཚེ་འདི་མི་རྟག་ཅིང་སྙིང་པོ་མེད་པ་ཞེ་ཕུགས་སུ་བཅུག་སྟེ་འཇིག་རྟེན་གྱི་འཁྲི་བ་བློས་བཏང་ལ་ཚེ་དང་སྒྲུབ་པ་སྙོམ་པར་བྱ་བའི་བློ་བསྐྱེད།

Part Three
Subsequent Ways to Continue the Training

This has six points:

General reasons for meditation training
Special training without separating meditation and postmeditation
Cutting through hindrances, sidetracks and strayings
Enhancing by transcending into nonarising
Developing strength through utilizing the conducts
How realization arises and the enhancement practices

General Reasons for Meditation Training

It is not enough that the meditation practice has taken birth; you must sustain it perfectly. Unless you sustain it after the meditation has arisen, you will either remain an ordinary person or you will exert yourself in other kinds of conceptual practices for gathering and purifying.[10] This would be straying from the true meaning, just as if the king would behave like his subjects or if a lion would join a pack of dogs.

To deal with this, since revulsion is like the feet or the guardian of your meditation practice, you should contemplate the suffering of samsara. Keeping in your innermost mind that this life is impermanent and without lasting substance, cut worldly ties and resolve to equalize life and practice.

མོས་གུས་སྒོམ་གྱི་མགོ་བོའམ་བོགས་འདོན་ལྟ་བུ་ཡིན་པས་བླ་མ་དང་བཀའ་བརྒྱུད་ལ་སངས་རྒྱས་དངོས་ཀྱི་འདུ་ཤེས་དང་མ་བྲལ་བར་རེ་ལྟོས་བཅས་ནས་གསོལ་བ་སྙིང་ནས་འདེབས།

དྲན་པ་སྒོམ་གྱི་བྱ་ར་བའམ་དངོས་གཞི་ཡིན་པས་ཐུན་གྱི་དུས་མིན་པ་གཞན་བློས་བཏང་མི་བྱ་བར་དུས་དང་གནས་སྐབས་ཐམས་ཅད་དུ་གནས་ལུགས་ཀྱི་དྲན་པ་དང་མ་བྲལ་བ་ལ་བསླབ།

སྒོམ་གྱི་ཕྲིན་ལས་སྙིང་རྗེ་ལ་བྱ་སྟེ་སེམས་ཅན་ཐམས་ཅད་ལ་བྱམས་སྙིང་རྗེ་བྱང་ཆུབ་ཀྱི་སེམས་སྒོམ་ཞིང་བསྔོ་བ་སྨོན་ལམ་གྱི་སྐྱབས་འོག་ཏུ་བཟུག།

རང་སྒོམ་མཐར་མ་ཕྱིན་པར་གཞན་ལ་སྟོན་པ་དང་སྤྲེལ་བའི་གཞན་དོན་ལྟར་སྣང་བདུད་ཀྱི་བར་ཆད་དུ་བཟུང་ལ་དབེན་པ་བསྟེན།

སྒོམ་གྱི་གོ་ཆ་ཁྲེལ་དང་ངོ་ཚ་ལ་བྱ་སྟེ་ནང་རང་སེམས་དཔང་པོར་བཞག་ཅིང་ཕྱི་ནས་བླ་མ་དཀོན་མཆོག་དང་མཆེད་གྲོགས་ཀྱིས་མི་ཁྲེལ་བར་ཡིད་ཆེས་པའི་རི་མཚམས་དང་འདག་སྦྱར་དང་སྒྲུབ་བཅད་སོགས་ཀྱི་སྒོ་ནས་བསྒོམ་པ་ལ་ནན་ཏན་བྱའོ།།

Since devotion is like the head or the enhancement of your meditation practice, entrust yourself fully and make sincere supplications to your guru and the Kagyü lineage masters, never parting from seeing them as buddhas in person.

Since mindfulness is the watchman or heart of your meditation practice, never forsake it, not only during sessions, but also train in keeping constant company by reminding yourself of the natural state at all times and in all situations.

Make compassion the activity of your meditation practice, so that you cultivate loving kindness, compassion and bodhichitta for all sentient beings and bring them under your protection with dedication and aspirations.

Until you have reached perfection in your meditation training, keep to secluded places and regard as Mara's obstacles the superficial acts of "benefiting others" by teaching and propagating the Dharma to them.

Make modesty and conscience the armor of your meditation practice, so that inwardly you take your own mind as witness, while outwardly you do not create any causes for displeasing your precious teacher or Dharma friends. Exert yourself in meditation practice by staying in strict mountain retreat, sealing off your room, keeping silent and so forth.

གཉིས་པ་ཁྱད་པར་མཉམ་རྗེས་སུ་སྒོམ་སྐྱོང་ཚུལ་ནི།

སྒོམ་སྟ་ཟིན་ཙམ་ནས་རྩེ་གཅིག་ཆེན་པོའི་བར་དུ་རང་ཁའི་མཉམ་རྗེས་ཙམ་ལས་མཉམ་རྗེས་མཚན་ཉིད་པ་མེད་པར་བཤད་ཅིང་།

འོན་ཀྱང་སྒོམ་སྐྱོང་བ་ལ་སྤྱིར་རང་རིག་གི་དྲན་པ་མ་ཡེངས་ན་ཐམས་ཅད་སྒོམ་ཡིན་པས་སྤང་བླང་མེད་ཀྱང་རྟོགས་པའི་མཉམ་རྗེས་མ་འདྲེས་ཀྱི་བར་དུ་ཐུན་གྱི་དངོས་གཞི་མཉམ་བཞག་ཏུ་བྱས་ལ་ངོ་བོ་རྩེ་གཅིག་ཏུ་སྐྱོང་བ་དང་།

ཐུན་མཚམས་སུ་རྗེས་ཐོབ་ཏུ་བྱས་ལ་རྟོག་པ་དང་སྣང་བ་ལམ་དུ་འཁྱེར་བ་སྒྲུབ་བརྒྱུད་ཕལ་ཆེར་གྱི་དགོངས་པར་གོ་ཞིག།

གང་ཟག་ཤེས་ཆེ་བ་ལ་རེ་ཞིག་སྒོམ་སྐྱེད་ཀྱང་འདི་ཆེ་སྣང་བས་དེ་ལྟར་བཤད་པར་བྱ་སྟེ་དེ་ལ། ངོ་བོའི་སྐྱོང་ཐབས་སོ་མ་རང་ཐང་ལྷུག་པ་གསུམ་ཏུ་བཞག་པར་བཤད་པ་ལས།

སོ་མ་ལ་ལུས་གནད་ཁོང་གློད་ངག་གནད་རླུང་མི་བཙོང་སེམས་གནད་གང་ལ་ཡང་རྟེན་མི་བཅའ་བར་རྩེས་གདབ་མེད་པར་བཞག།

རང་ཐང་ལ་སེམས་རང་ལུགས་སུ་བཞག་ངོས་བཟུང་མེད་པར་བཞག་མ་ཡེངས་པར་བཞག།

Special Training without Separating Meditation and Postmeditation

From when you have *taken hold of the meditation* until the greater One-Pointedness, it is taught that you only have an ordinary type of meditation state and postmeditation, not the authentic kind. Nevertheless, everything is meditation training if your naturally aware presence of mind does not wander while practicing.

So, although you may be free from accepting and rejecting, until you succeed in intermingling the meditation and postmeditation of realization, you should make the meditation state the main part of your session and sustain your essence one-pointedly.[11] During the breaks, focus on the postmeditation and make use of thoughts and perceptions. Understand this to be the intent of most of the Practice Lineages. This is also how it appears for most people, even though they may have *given birth to the meditation*; so this is how it should be taught.[12]

As for sustaining the essence, it is taught that you should remain in these three manners: fresh, artless and unbound.

To be fresh, the key point of body is to relax deeply from within. The key point of speech is not to force your breathing. The key point of mind is to remain unconcerned and without taking anything as support.

To be artless, leave your mind as it naturally is, leave it without being a definable entity and remain undistracted.

ལྷུག་པ་ལ་དགག་སྒྲུབ་མེད་པར་བཞག་འབད་རྩོལ་མེད་པར་བཞག་ཚོགས་དྲུག་རང་བབས་སུ་བཞག་པ་སྐྱེ་གནད་དགུར་ཕྱི་བའམ།

རྩིས་གདབ་མེད་པར་རང་ལུགས་སོ་མར་བཞག།

དགག་སྒྲུབ་ཀྱིས་མ་བཅོས་པར་རང་གར་བཞག།

རྩོལ་སྒྲུབ་མི་བྱ་བར་ལྷུག་པར་བཞག་པ་སྐྱེ་གནད་གསུམ་དང་ལྡན་པར་བྱའོ།།

དེ་དག་དཔེར་ན། ནམ་མཁའ་ལྟར་དཔངས་བསྟོད་དེ་སྟང་བ་གུ་ཡངས་སང་ངེ་བཞག།

ས་གཞི་ལྟར་རྒྱ་བསྐྱེད་དེ་དྲན་པ་ཁྱབ་ཆེར་བཞག།

རི་བོ་ལྟར་ལྷུན་ཕབ་ལ་སེམས་གཡོ་འགྱུལ་མེད་པར་བཞག།

མར་མེ་ལྟར་གསལ་བ་སྟོང་ལ་རིག་པ་གསལ་སིང་ངེ་བཞག།

མན་ཤེལ་ལྟར་དྲི་མ་སྤངས་ལ་ཤེས་པ་རྟོག་མེད་དུ་དྭངས་སང་ངེ་བཞག་པ་སྐྱེ་ལྔའམ།

སྤྲིན་མེད་པའི་ནམ་མཁའ་སྒྲིབ་གཡོགས་དང་བྲལ་བ་ལྟར་ངོས་བཟུང་མེད་པར་གུ་ཡངས་སང་ངེ་བཞག།

རླབས་དང་བྲལ་བའི་རྒྱ་མཚོ་མི་གཡོ་བ་ལྟར་རྟོག་མེད་དུ་མ་ཡེངས་པར་ལྷམ་མེ་བཞག།

To be unbound, remain free from accepting and rejecting, remain effortless and leave the six sense impressions in naturalness.

In this way, nine essential points are listed. Phrased differently, you should possess these three key points:

Remain fresh in unconcerned naturalness.
Remain artless and uncontrived without judging.
Remain unbound and uninvolved in striving.

❧

Here are five analogies for this:

Elevate your experience and remain wide-open like the sky.
Expand your mindfulness and remain pervasive like the earth.
Steady your attention and remain unshakable like a mountain.
Brighten your awareness and remain shining like a flame.
Clear your thoughtfree wakefulness and remain lucid like a crystal.

❧

Additionally, remain composed like in these three examples:

Unobscured like a cloudless sky, remain in a lucid and intangable openness.
Unmoving like the ocean free of waves, remain in

རླུང་གིས་མ་བསྐྱོད་པའི་མར་མེ་གསལ་འགྲིབ་མེད་པ་ལྟར་གསལ་སིང་ངེ་ཡེ་རེ་བཞག་པ་སྟེ་དཔེ་གསུམ་ལྟར་མཉམ་པར་བཞག་གོ།།

དེ་ཡང་དང་པོར་རྩོལ་སྒྲུབ་དང་བྲལ་བས་ལུས་སེམས་ཁོང་གློད། བར་དུ་ཚོམ་ཚོམ་མི་བྱ་བར་སོ་མ་མ་བཅོས་པར་བཞག། ཐ་མར་བྱུང་ཚོར་ཐམས་ཅད་སྐྱེ་མེད་རང་གྲོལ་དུ་ཐག་བཅད་དེ་སྐྱོང་བར་བཤད་ལ།

ལུས་ཁོང་གློད་པ་ནི་ལུས་ཤིན་ཏུ་སྒྲིམ་ཞིང་གཟུན་པའི་རྩོལ་བ་གློད་པ་ཡིན་གྱི། ལུས་གནད་ཀྱི་ཚུལ་ཐམས་ཅད་འདོར་བ་མིན་པས་ལུས་གནད་རང་བབས་ནི་ཤིན་ཏུ་གལ་ཆེའོ།།

མ་བཅོས་པ་ལྷུག་པར་འཇོག་པ་ཡང་དམིགས་བཅས་ཀྱི་དགག་སྒྲུབ་དང་ཞེ་འདོད་མི་བྱ་བ་ཡིན་གྱི། ལུང་མ་བསྟན་ཏུ་སོང་བ་དང་ཉམས་འལ་འོལ་གྱིས་གཡོགས་པའི་ལར་གཏོང་བ་མིན་པས་དྲན་རིག་སལ་ལེ་བའི་སེམས་རྗེན་པར་བསྐྱང་ངོ་། བྱུང་ཚོར་སྐྱེ་མེད་དུ་ཐག་བཅད་པ་ཡང་རང་རིག་གི་དྲན་པས་བཟུང་མ་ཐག་གང་སྣང་སྐྱེ་འགག་གནས་གསུམ་གྱི་ངོ་བོར་མ་གྲུབ་པར་གྲོལ་བ་དེ་ཉིད་ཡིན་གྱི། སྐྱེ་མེད་རང་གྲོལ་དུ་ཀུན་ཏུ་རྟོག་པས་རྒྱུས་འདེབས་པ་མིན་པས་ངོས་བཟུང་མེད་པར་བསྐྱང་ངོ་།

ཤེས་པ་ལ་བྱིང་རྒོད་ཀྱིས་མཉམ་པར་བཞག་མ་བདེ་ན་སོ་སོའི་གནད་བཅོས་ལ་རེ་ཤིག་མདུང་བྲི་ཁྲུང་དུ་བཙུག་པ་ལྟར་རྩེ་གཅིག་ཏུ་སྐྱོང་དགོས་པ་ཡིན་ནོ།།

complete ease, undistracted by thought.
Unchanging and brilliant like a flame undisturbed
by the wind, remain utterly clear and bright.

Here is how it is taught: First, suspend all effort to deeply relax body and mind. Next, let be in uncontrived freshness without indecision. Finally, maintain the practice after resolving that all perceptions are nonarising and naturally freed.

To 'deeply relax the body' means simply to release the effort of excessively tightening or tensing the body, but not to cast away all the key points of physical posture. Naturalness, therefore, is the most important key point of body.

To 'let be uncontrived and unbound' means simply to refrain from ambitious and goal-oriented judging, while not becoming apathetic or obscured by a hazy meditation-mood. Therefore, maintain the naked state of a lucid presence of mind.

To 'resolve that perceptions are nonarising' means simply that every perception dissolves — in the sense of being free from an identity that arises, remains or ceases — the very moment it is embraced by your naturally aware presence of mind. It does not mean to label it with the concept 'nonarising self-liberation'. Therefore, train in not pinpointing anything.[13]

If dullness and agitation make it unwieldy to keep your mind composed, adjust them with their respective key

དེས་སྐྱོ་ན་ཐུན་མཚམས་སོགས་རྗེས་ཐོབ་ཐམས་ཅད་དུ་རང་རིག་གི་དྲན་པ་རྒྱུན་ཆགས་སུ་བྱས་ཏེ་རྣམ་རྟོག་དང་སྣང་བའི་འཆར་སྒོ་ཅི་སྣང་ཅི་ཤར་དེ་མ་ཡེངས་པར་སྐྱོང་ལ།

དཔེར་ན་རྫི་བོ་མཁས་པས་ཕྱུགས་སྐྱོང་བ་ལྟ་བུ་སྟེ། ཕྱུགས་རྣམས་ཅི་བདེར་ཡན་ཡང་བསྲུ་བ་སོགས་མི་དགོས་པར་མིག་ལམ་ནས་མ་བོར་བས་ཆོག་པ་ལྟར།

རྣམ་རྟོག་དང་ཚོགས་དྲུག་གི་སྣང་བ་ཅི་ཤར་ཅི་སྣང་ཐམས་ཅད་དགག་པའམ་བཀག་མི་དགོས་པར། རང་རིག་གི་དྲན་པ་གཞུང་བསྲངས་ཏེ་གང་ཤར་ངོས་བཟུང་མེད་པར་ལྷུག་པར་སྐྱོང་བ།

དེ་ཡང་སྤྱོད་ལམ་རྣམ་བཞི་ལ་སོགས་པར་མ་ཡེངས་པའི་དྲན་པ་ས་ལེ་བ་རྒྱུན་ཆགས་སུ་བརྟེན་པས། དང་པོར་ཡེངས་པ་ཤས་ཆེ་ནའང་རིམ་པས་ཤུགས་འབྱུང་གི་དྲན་པ་འཕེལ་ཏེ་རྟོག་པ་དང་སྣང་བ་ཕལ་ཆེར་གསལ་སྟོང་དུ་ལྷང་ལྷང་འཆར་ལ། ཅི་ནས་ཀྱང་སྐྱོང་དཀའ་ན་མཉམ་བཞག་གི་ངང་ནས་རྟོག་སྣང་གང་ཡང་རུང་བ་འཆར་དུ་བཅུག་ལ་དེའི་ངོ་བོ་བལྟ་བ་སོགས་བྱས་ཏེ་གཏན་ལ་ཕབ་ནས་གོང་ལྟར་སྐྱོང་།

མཉམ་རྗེས་སྐྱོང་ཚུལ་དེ་ལྟར་འབད་པས་ཅི་ཞིག་ན་ཐམས་ཅད་རང་རིག་གི་དྲན་པས་ཁྱབ་སྟེ་རྟོག་སྣང་ཅི་ཤར་ཅི་སྣང་ཐམས་ཅད་ཤར་ཙམ་སྣང་ཙམ་ཉིད་ནས་གསལ་སྟོང་ངོས་བཟུང་མེད་པ་འཆར་ཞིང་།

points. For a while, train in being one-pointed, as firm as a stake driven into the ground.

When you grow weary of this, keep a constant, naturally aware presence of mind during the breaks and during all instances of postmeditation, and maintain it undistractedly, no matter what thought or perception occurs.

This is like the example of a competent herdsman tending to his cattle. They are allowed to roam freely. He does not have to keep bringing them together. It is enough to simply not lose sight of them. Similarly, no matter which thought or perception occurs, you do not need to block it or keep it under control. Rather, promote a naturally aware presence of mind and thus continue the practice with unbound ease without pinpointing whatever is experienced.

To explain further, during the four types of daily activities and so forth, continuously maintain an undistracted and lucid presence of mind. By doing so, even though distraction is compelling at first, a spontaneous presence of mind gradually expands, so that you experience nearly all thoughts and perceptions as a vivid state of aware emptiness.

If this is downright hard to maintain, let a thought or perception unfold within the state of composure and look into its identity to settle it. Then continue in the manner above.

When you persevere in this training during composure and postmeditation, there will come a point when everything is embraced with the naturally aware presence of

མཉམ་བཞག་ཏུ་ངོ་བོ་རྩེ་གཅིག་ཏུ་སྐྱོང་བ་དང་རྗེས་ཐོབ་ཏུ་རྟོག་སྣང་དྲན་པས་སྐྱོང་བ་གཉིས་ངོ་བོ་ཁྱད་མེད་པ་འབྱུང་ལ།

བདེ་གསལ་མི་རྟོག་པའི་ཉམས་སྲབ་མཐུག་སྣ་ཚོགས་ཀྱང་འབྱུང་ངོ་།

ཉམས་དང་འགྲོགས་ན་གནས་ལུགས་ལ་སྒྲིབ་པས་དྲན་རིག་ངར་བསྐྱེད་ཏུར་ཕྱུང་ལ་ཡང་དང་ཡང་དུ་ཤེས་པ་ཉམས་ཀྱི་རྣན་དང་ཕྲལ་ཏེ་སོ་མ་རྗེན་པ་སྐྱོང་བར་བྱའོ།།

གསུམ་པ་གེགས་སེལ་ས་དང་གོལ་ས་བཅད་པ་ནི།

ཐོས་པ་དམན་ཞིང་བླ་མ་བསྟེན་ཡུན་ཐུང་བ་དག་ལ་གོ་བ་དང་ཉམས་ལ་བརྟེན་ནས་ཤོར་གོལ་འབྱུང་ཉེན་ཆེ་སྟེ།

དེ་ཡང་སྟོང་ཉིད་ལ་ཤོར་ས་བཞིར་བཤད་པའི་ཤེས་བྱའི་གཤིས་ལ་ཤོར་བ་ལ།

སྒོམ་སྣང་སྟོང་དབྱེར་མེད་རྣམ་ཀུན་མཆོག་ལྡན་གྱི་གནད་མ་རིག་པར་སྐྱོན་ཡོན་གང་གིས་ཀྱང་མི་དགོས་ཤིང་བདེན་པར་མ་གྲུབ་པའི་སྟོང་པ་ཡིན་སྙམ་དུ་དགེ་སྡིག་ཁྱད་དུ་གསོད་པ་ཡི་ཤོར་དང་།

mind. This is when thoughts and perceptions, no matter how they occur, are all experienced, the very moment they are thought or perceived, as an aware emptiness in which nothing can be pinpointed.

These two — maintaining the essence one-pointedly during composure and tending thoughts and perceptions with mindfulness during postmeditation — are essentially no different. You will also have a variety of heavy and light meditation-moods of bliss, clarity and nonthought.

If you keep company with these moods, they will obscure the natural state. So, bring forth a sharp and alert mindful presence. Again and again, extricate your mind when immersed in the meditation-moods. Maintain the fresh and naked state.

Cutting through Hindrances, Sidetracks and Straying

Third, for people of little learning, who have only spent a short time following their master, there is a great risk of getting involved in sidetracks and strayings due to intellectual understanding and meditative moods.

Among the described four types of strayings concerning emptiness, the straying with regard to the nature of knowables has two aspects:

Instead of recognizing the essential point of the training to be the indivisible unity of perception and emptiness endowed with the supreme of all aspects, the basic straying is to disregard good and evil by thinking it is an unreal

སྒོམ་གྱི་ངོ་བོའི་དོན་ཇི་ལྟར་བར་གོ་ཞིང་དེའི་རྩལ་བཤད་ཤེས་ཀྱང་རང་གི་མྱོང་ཐོག་ཏུ་མ་ཁེལ་བའི་འཁྲུལ་ཤོར་གཉིས།

ལམ་ཏུ་ཤོར་བ་ལ་སྒོམ་ལམ་འབྲས་དབྱེར་མེད་འབྲས་བུ་རང་ཆས་སུ་ཡོད་པར་མ་རིག་པར་སྒོམ་ལ་ལམ་བྱས་ནས་འབྲས་བུ་གཞན་ཞིག་ཐོབ་པར་འདོད་པ་ཡི་ཤོར་དང་།

སྒོམ་ཇི་ལྟར་བར་རང་ལ་ཡོད་ཀྱང་དེ་ལ་བློ་མ་ཁེལ་བར་དེ་བས་ལྷག་པ་ཡོད་དུ་རེ་ནས་གཞན་དུ་ཚོལ་བའམ་སྒོམ་དེ་ཉིད་ལ་ལྷག་པ་བསྣན་ནས་བསྒོམ་པ་འཁྲུལ་ཤོར་གཉིས།

གཉེན་པོར་ཤོར་བ་ལ་སྒོམ་སྣང་གཉེན་དབྱེར་མེད་རང་ངོ་རང་རིག་པས་སྣང་བྱ་ཉིད་གཉེན་པོར་འཆར་བ་མ་རིག་པར་སྣང་བྱ་ཉོན་མོངས་དང་སྒོམ་སོ་སོར་བཟུང་སྟེ་ཉོན་མོངས་ཀྱི་གཉེན་པོར་སྒོམ་བྱེད་པ་ཡི་ཤོར་དང་།

རྣམ་རྟོག་འགྲོ་བའམ་གཞན་ཡང་རྐྱེན་དང་འཕྲད་པའི་ཚེ་དེ་ཉིད་བཤིག་ནས་སྒོམ་དུ་འཇོག་པ་འཁྲུལ་ཤོར་གཉིས།

empty state in which faults and qualities are totally inconsequential. Although the meditator has understood the exact meaning of the essential training and is able to explain it, the temporary straying is to fail to bring it into personal experience.

❧

Straying with regard to the path has two aspects:

Instead of recognizing that the training is the indivisible unity of path and fruition and that this fruition is present as a natural possession, the basic straying is to believe that the path is the training, while the fruition will be attained at another point.

Although the meditator does possess the exact training, the temporary straying is to distrust it and seek it elsewhere hoping for something superior or to meditate while adding something better.

❧

Straying with regard to the remedy has two aspects:

Instead of recognizing the training as the indivisible unity of discard and remedy, and that by knowing your natural face the discard becomes its own remedy, the basic straying is to regard the emotion to be discarded and the training as separate and so to use the training as a remedy against the emotion.

Whenever a thought moves or when encountering a difficult situation, the temporary straying is (to believe that) one can only be composed in meditation after the difficulty has been overcome.

❧

རྒྱས་འདེབས་སུ་ཤོར་བ་ལ། སྒོམ་ཐབས་ཤེས་དབྱེར་མེད་ཆོས་ཐམས་ཅད་ངོ་བོ་ཉིད་དུ་གནས་པ་མ་རིག་པར་དམིགས་བཅས་ལ་རང་བཞིན་མ་གྲུབ་པར་རྒྱས་འདེབས་པ་ཡི་ཤོར་དང་།

སྒོམ་ལམ་དུ་མ་བསླངས་པར་ཕྱི་སྣགས་བྱས་ལ་སྒོམ་ཡིན་སྙམ་དུ་རྒྱས་འདེབས་པའམ་སྤུ་མ་མ་ཉན་སླར་སྒོམ་སྙམ་དུ་རྣམ་རྟོག་སྒོམ་གྱིས་བཅད་པ་ལྷ་བུའི་འཕྲུལ་ཤོར་གཉིས་ཏེ།

འདིས་མཚོན་པ་མཐའ་དག་སྒོམ་གྱི་ཤོར་ས་ཡིན་ལ། ཤོར་བ་འགའ་ཞིག་གིས་ངན་སོང་དུ་ལྟུང་བ་ཡོད་ཅིང་གཞན་ཡང་སྒོམ་ལ་སྨྲོང་བ་རྣུས་མི་ཐོན་པའི་བློ་དྲེད་ཅན་དུ་འགྱུར་བས་མ་ཤོར་བ་གལ་ཆེའོ།།

གོལ་ས་ནི། སྤྱིར་སྒོམ་བསྐྱངས་པས་བདེ་བསལ་མི་རྟོག་པའི་ཉམས་ཀྱི་བྱེ་བྲག་མཐའ་ཡས་པ་འཆར་ཞིང་།

ཁྱད་པར་སྒྲུབ་པ་པོ་རྩ་ཐིག་རླུང་གསུམ་བཟང་བ་དང་རྣམ་གཡེང་དང་ལེ་ལོས་བར་མ་བཅད་པར་སྒོམ་ལ་འཇུར་བ་དག་ལ་ཉམས་ཀྱི་རིགས་ངོ་མཚར་ཞིང་བརྗོད་ཀྱིས་མི་ལང་བ་སྐྱེ་ལ། སྒོམ་དང་བྱ་བ་གཞན་བསྲེས་ནས་བསྒོམ་པ་ལ་ཉམས་བག་རེ་ལས་མི་འབྱུང་ངོ་།

གང་ལྟར་ནའང་བདེ་ཉམས་ལ་ལུས་བདེ་བས་ཁྱབ་པ་དང་།

Straying with regard to generalization has two aspects:

Instead of recognizing that the training is the indivisible unity of means and knowledge and that all phenomena are the essence itself, the basic straying is to generalize with conceptual focus that they are devoid of self-nature.

Rather than putting the training to use, the temporary straying is to generalize by wanting to recreate a past experience. Or, it could be to believe that meditation should interrupt thoughts: "I am dissatisfied with the present state. I must create a better one later!"[14]

As illustrated, these are examples for strayings from the meditation training. Some types of straying can send you to the lower realms or turn you into an unfeeling person who never gained any thorough experience in practice. Therefore, it is essential not to stray.

Sidetracks

Generally speaking, while continuing the training you will encounter myriad different meditation-moods of bliss, clarity and nonthought. In particular, practitioners who have excellent channels, energies and essences, or devote themselves vigorously to the practice without being interrupted by laziness and distractions, will have wondrous meditation experiences of a variety that defies description. Those who practice while intermingling their practice with other activities will only encounter tiny bits of such meditative states.

ཚ་གྲང་གི་རེག་པ་ཡང་བདེ་བར་འཆར་བ་དང་ལུས་ཡོད་མེད་མི་ཚོར་བར་བདེ་བ་དང་དགའ་ཞིང་རྐྱོད་འདོད་པ་སོགས་དང་སེམས་སྤྲོ་བ་དང་སྐྱིད་སྣང་འཆར་བ་དང་བློ་བདེ་ཞིང་འབོལ་བ་དང་ཉིན་མཚན་ངོ་མི་ཤེས་པ་ཙམ་གྱི་བདེ་བ་སྣ་ཚོགས་པ་འབྱུང་། གསལ་ཉམས་ལ་སེམས་དྭངས་བ་དང་སྣང་བ་ཐམས་ཅད་གསལ་བ་དང་མཚན་མོ་ཡང་ཉེ་རིང་གི་དངོས་པོ་ཐམས་ཅད་རིག་པ་དང་འོད་གསལ་བའི་སྣང་བ་སོགས་དང་གཞན་སེམས་ཤེས་པ་སྙམ་བྱེད་པ་སོགས་སྣ་ཚོགས་འབྱུང་།

མི་རྟོག་པའི་ཉམས་ལ་སྟོང་གཟུགས་ཀྱི་རྟགས་སྣ་ཚོགས་འཆར་བ་དང་ཐམས་ཅད་ལ་སྟོང་པའི་འཛིན་སྟངས་སྐྱེ་བ་དང་། སྣང་བ་བཀག་མེད་དུ་རང་བཞིན་མེད་པར་སྣང་བ་དང་རང་དང་སྣང་བ་སྟོང་པར་འཆར་བ་དང་སྟོང་པའི་ངེས་ཤེས་སྐྱེ་བ་སོགས་སྣ་ཚོགས་འབྱུང་ངོ་།

བདེ་གསལ་མི་རྟོག་པ་གསུམ་གའི་ཉམས་སམ་ཉམས་ཕྱོགས་རེ་བ་གང་ཡིན་ཡང་འདྲ་སྟེ། ཉམས་དེ་དག་ལ་མཆོག་ཏུ་བཟུང་ནས་ཉམས་ཀྱིས་དགྲིས་པའི་སྒོམ་དེ་བྱུང་ན་དགའ་མི་དགའ་བར་ཆེད་དུ་བསྐྱང་ན། བདེ་བས་འདོད་ཁམས་གསལ་བས་གཟུགས་ཁམས་མི་རྟོག་པས་གཟུགས་མེད་ཁམས་སུ་སྐྱེ་བའི་རྒྱུ་བྱེད་ལ།

ཞེན་འཛིན་མེད་ཀྱང་ཉམས་ཀྱིས་དགྲིས་པའི་སྒོམ་དེས་ཉན་རང་གི་གོ་འཕང་སྒྲུབ་ཅིང་ངན་འགྲོའི་སྡུག་བསྔལ་ལས་ངལ་གསོ་ཙམ་འཐོབ་ཀྱི་རྫོགས་པའི་སངས་རྒྱས་ཐོབ་པ་ལ་ཅུང་ཟད་ཀྱང་ནུད་ཐུབ་པ་དཀའོ།།

Regardless, the bliss experience can be of many different types. These include your body feeling permeated by bliss — even heat and cold feel pleasant; you do not notice whether or not you have a body; you feel so thrilled and joyful that you want to break out laughing; you are delighted and overjoyed, free and easy; or you do not notice whether it is day or night.

The clarity experience can be of various kinds. These include having a lucid state of mind, all perceptions becoming crystal-clear, seeing close and distant things even at night, seeing displays of luminosity, having the feeling of knowing other people's minds, and so forth.

The experience of nonthought has a variety of types. These include seeing the various signs of 'empty forms', having the feeling that everything is empty, seeing perceptions as insubstantial and devoid of self-nature, seeing oneself and perceptions as empty, feeling certain of emptiness, and so forth.

Whether it is one of these three meditative moods — bliss, clarity and nonthought — in combination or a part of any of them, you might cling to these meditative experiences as being paramount and train in a way that is fettered by them, by being happy when they come and unhappy when they do not. If such is the case, bliss will cause rebirth in the Desire Realms, clarity in the Form Realms, and nonthought in the Formless Realms.

Even if you are not clinging to these meditative moods, a meditation training that is fettered by them will make you generate the states of the shravakas and pratyeka-

གཞན་ཡང་ཤེས་རབ་དམན་ཞིང་ཐོས་པ་ཆུང་ན།

ངོ་བོ་གཞུག་མ་སྐྱོང་བ་ལས་ལོག་ནས་སྒོམ་ཕྱོགས་རེ་བ་དང་གནས་པ་འཐུག་པོ་དང་ཉམས་འལ་འོལ་དང་གཞུག་མ་རབ་རིབ་ཅན་གྱི་ཁར་འཕོར་བ་འོང་ངོ་།

དེས་ན་གོལ་ས་འགའ་ཞིག་གིས་ངན་འགྲོར་སྐྱེ་དོགས་ཡོད་ལ་གཞན་དག་ཀྱང་སྲིད་པའི་བདེ་བ་སྒྲུབ་ནུས་པ་ཙམ་ལས་མེད་དེ།

དཔེར་ན་ཤར་དུ་འགྲོ་བར་འདོད་པ་ལ་ནུབ་དང་བྱང་དུ་སོང་བ་ལྟར་དོན་འཆུགས་པ་ཡིན་ནོ།།

ཉམས་ལ་ཞི་གནས་ཀྱི་ཉམས་དང་ལྷག་མཐོང་གི་ཉམས་དང་རྟོགས་པའི་རང་ཉམས་གསུམ་ཡོད་པའི་ཕྱི་མ་གོལ་སར་མི་འཛིན་ཞིང་བར་པ་ཡང་ཞེན་མེད་དུ་སྒོམ་ཐད་ཀར་བསྐྱངས་པས་ཉམས་རང་སར་དག་ནས་བོགས་ཐོན་ལ།

འོན་ཀྱང་ཉམས་བྲིངས་ཅན་ཕལ་ཆེར་དགེ་སྦྱོར་ན་འཕར་བའི་གེགས་སུ་འགྱུར་ཞིང་གནས་ལུགས་ལ་སྒྲིབ་པས།

ཐབས་སྣ་ཚོགས་པས་ཉམས་བཤིག་ནས་བསྒོམ་པ་ཆོད་ཆེ་བ་ཡིན་ནོ།

buddhas, and you will attain nothing but a rest from the sufferings of the lower realms. It will hardly enable you to attain buddhahood, not even in the slightest.

Furthermore, people whose intelligence is weak and who have received few teachings can misunderstand the training in the original essence. They will promote either an imperfect training, a dense type of calm, a hazy meditation-mood, or detour into a distorted version of the natural state.

Therefore, some sidetracks have the danger of leading to rebirth in the lower realms, while others can provide nothing more than a samsaric state of well-being. Like the example of walking to the west or north, when intending to go east, the aim is mistaken.

༄

As for meditative experiences, there are three types which are connected to shamatha, vipashyana and the actual experience of realization. Among these three, the last is not regarded as a straying. The second, when the training is sustained with immediacy and free from clinging, will bring progress after the meditative moods have naturally dissolved.

Nevertheless, meditative experiences that involve trance-like immersion are, for the most part, hindrances for making headway in spiritual practice and obscure the natural state. It will be most effective to train after destroying these meditation-moods with various methods.

༄ བཞི་པ་སྐྱེ་མེད་དུ་ལ་བཟླས་ཏེ་བོགས་འབྱུང་བ་ལ་ལྔ།

ལ་བཟླ་བའི་དུས་ཚོད།

རྟོག་པ་དང་སྣང་བ་རྒྱུད་གཅོད་པ།

སྒོམ་དང་སྒོམ་མཁན་གྱི་སེམས་རྒྱུད་གཅོད་པ།

སྐྱེ་མེད་ཟང་ཐལ་དུ་ལ་བཟླ་བ་དངོས།

མཉམ་རྗེས་ཉིན་མཚན་རྣམས་བསྲེ་བའོ།།

དང་པོ་ནི། སྒྲུབ་པ་པོ་བདེ་གསལ་མི་རྟོག་པའི་ཉམས་འཕྲུག་པོ་དག་ནས་སེམས་གསལ་དྭངས་ཐོན་ཏེ་གསལ་སྟོང་ནམ་མཁའ་ལྟ་བུའི་སྒོམ་འཁོར་ཡུག་ཏུ་སོང་བའམ། ཉིན་སྣང་ཤེས་ཚེ་བ་ཁོར་ཡུག་ཏུ་འགྲོ་ཞིང་རྟོག་པ་འགྱུ་ཐོག་ཏུ་དྲན་པས་ནམ་ཟིན་གསལ་སྟོང་སང་དེ་ཚོགས་དྲུག་གི་སྣང་ཐོག་ཏུ་དྲན་པས་ནམ་ཟིན་སྣང་སྟོང་ལྷང་དེ་འཆར་ཞིང་རྟོག་སྣང་གི་ཐོག་ཏུ་ངེས་ཤེས་ཐག་ཆོད་སྐྱེས་པའི་ཚེ་ལ་བཟླའོ།།

ལ་བཟླ་སྐབས་ན་སྒྲོང་བ་མི་ཐོན་པར་གོ་ཡུལ་ལ་བརྟེན་པའི་དྲེད་པོ་ཁའི་ལྟ་བ་མཐོ་བ་ཞིག་འབྱུང་ལ། ཏ་ཙང་འཕྱིས་ན་སྐལ་བ་ཅན་དག་ཉམས་སྒྲོང་གི་ཞེན་འཛིན་རང་དག་ལ་སོང་ནས་རྟོགས་པ་འཁོར་ཡུག་ཏུ་གྲོལ་བ་མང་ཡང་། འགའ་ཞིག་ལ་བཟང་རྟོག་ངེས་ཤེས་ཀྱི་འཛིན་པ་ཆེར་སོང་ནས་དགེ་སྦྱོར་ལ་མཐོ་དམན་སྣ་ཚོགས་འོང་བ་ཡིན་ནོ།།

Enhancing by Transcending into Nonarising

This has five parts:
The time for transcending
Investigating thoughts and perceptions
Investigating the meditation and the meditating mind
The actual transcending into nonarising openness
Mingling meditation and postmeditation, day and night

The Time for Transcending

This is when the practitioner's dense meditation-moods of bliss, clarity and nonthought have dissolved. His mind has cleared up to such an extent that the meditation training in space-like aware emptiness has become constant. Or, it is when the daytime experience for the most part has become constant. It is whenever a thought's movement is embraced by mindfulness, so it becomes a lucid aware emptiness, and whenever the perceptions of the six senses are embraced by mindfulness, they become vivid empty perceptions. When you thus find a decisive certainty within thoughts and perceptions it is the time for transcending.

If the transcending takes place too soon, you will miss the real experience and instead become an insensitive intellectual spouting forth the words of a "high view". If too late, even though there may be many fortunate people who dissolve their clinging to experiences and are liberated into steady realization, others may intensify their clinging to

གཉིས་པ་ནི། སྔོན་འགྲོ་སྤྱི་དང་ཁྱད་པར་བླ་མའི་རྣལ་འབྱོར་གྱི་ཚེ་མོས་གུས་ཀྱི་གདུང་ཤུགས་དྲག་པོས་སྣང་སྲིད་ཆོས་སྐུར་འཆར་བར་གསོལ་བ་འདེབས་པ་ལ་འབད་ཅིང་ངོ་བོའི་བཞག་ཐབས་སྔར་བཤད་པ་ལྟར་རྩེ་གཅིག་ཏུ་བསྐྱངས་ཏེ་སེམས་དྭངས་སྙིགས་ཕྱེད་པ་དང་། སེམས་མ་ཡེངས་ཤིང་གུ་ཡངས་སང་ངེ་བའི་ངང་ནས་རྣམ་རྟོག་ཕྲ་རགས་དུ་མ་སྤྲོས་ཏེ་དེ་ལ་འཛིན་མེད་དུ་བལྟ་ཞིང་ཕྲ་རགས་དེ་ལ་ཁྱད་པར་ཅི་འདུག་བལྟ།

དེ་དང་སེམས་གནས་པའི་ངོ་བོ་ལ་ཁྱད་པར་ཅི་འདུག་བལྟ། དེ་བཞིན་དུ་བདེ་སྡུག་དང་ཉོན་མོངས་པ་དུག་གསུམ་གྱི་རྟོག་པ་སོགས་རྟོག་པ་སྣ་མང་པོ་ཞིག་ལ་བལྟ། རེས་རྟོག་པ་དགག་རེས་མང་དུ་སྤྲོ་རེས་རྒྱུན་འདེད་བྱ་བ་སོགས་སྣ་ཚོགས་པ་བྱས་ལ་བལྟ། ཕྱི་རོལ་གྱི་སྣང་བ་མཛེས་མི་མཛེས་སྙན་མི་སྙན་ཕྲ་རགས་སྣ་ཚོགས་ལ་བལྟ།

ལུས་ཀྱི་རྣམ་འགྱུར་སྣ་ཚོགས་དང་མིག་འབྲེད་འཛུམ་གཡས་ལྟ་གཡོན་ལྟ་ལ་སོགས་པའི་སྒོ་ནས་སྣང་བའི་འཆར་ལུགས་མི་འདྲ་བ་སྣ་ཚོགས་འཆར་དུ་བཅུག་ལ་དེ་དག་ལ་ཁྱད་པར་ཅི་འདུག་བལྟ།

དེ་དག་དང་སེམས་ཀྱི་ངོ་བོ་ལ་ཁྱད་པར་ཅི་འདུག་བལྟ་བ་ཞག་འགའ་བྱེད་དུ་བཅུག་ལ་ཐག་ཆོད་ཀྱི་མྱོང་བ་སྐྱེས་པ་དང་།

སྔར་བཤད་པ་ལྟར་རྣམ་རྟོག་དང་སྣང་བའི་ངོ་སྤྲོད་གསལ་འདེབས་བྱས་ཏེ་ངེས་ཤེས་བསྐྱེད་དོ།།

noble thoughts and conviction and get involved in various levels of virtuous activities.

Investigating Thoughts and Perceptions

During the preliminary practices in general and the guru yoga in particular, you should exert yourself in supplicating with deep-felt and sincere devotion that all that appears and exists may dawn as dharmakaya. Sustain one-pointedly the essential meditation method as explained earlier, and thus clarify your mind. Without getting distracted, remain wide-open and lucid. Within that state let various gross and subtle thoughts arise and, while looking into them without clinging, see whether there is any difference between the gross and subtle. See whether there is any difference between their identity and the identity of the calm state of mind.

In the same way, look into the various types of thoughts such as joy and sorrow, as well as the thoughts of the three poisons. Create different types of thought activity so that you sometimes look while stopping them, sometimes while thinking even more, sometimes while chasing after them and so forth.

Look into the various perceptions of external things, beautiful or ugly, pleasant or unpleasant. Let perceptions take place in varied ways through dissimilar physical expressions, opening and closing your eyes, looking right and left, and see whether there is any difference between them.

གསུམ་པ་ནི། སྒོམ་གྱི་ངོ་བོ་དེ་སྐྱེ་འགག་ངོས་བཟུང་མེད་པ་བློ་འདས་ཡིན་སླམ་པས་མི་ཆོག་པས་སེམས་མ་ཡེངས་ཤིང་གུ་ཡངས་སང་ངེ་བའི་ངང་ནས་སྒོམ་གྱི་ངོ་བོ་ལ་འཛིན་མེད་དུ་ལྟང་བལྟས་ལ་ཅི་འདྲ་འདུག་ཡང་ཡང་བལྟ།

དེ་བཞིན་དུ་སྒོམ་མཁན་གྱི་ཤེས་པ་དང་ང་དང་བདག་ཏུ་འཛིན་མཁན་གྱི་ཤེས་པ་ལ་ཡང་ཡང་བལྟ།

གཞན་ཡང་འདས་པ་དང་མ་འོངས་པ་དང་ད་ལྟའི་སེམས་གསུམ་ལ་ཁྱད་པར་ཅི་འདུག།

འདས་པའི་སེམས་གར་སོང་མ་འོངས་པའི་སེམས་གང་ལས་བྱུང་ད་ལྟའི་སེམས་ཧ་ལྟ་བུ་འདུག་བལྟ་ཞིང་ཞག་འགའ་སྐྲོ་འདོགས་གཅོད་དུ་བཙུག་ལ་ཐག་ཆོད་ཀྱི་མྱོང་བ་སྐྱེས་པ་དང་།

བསྒོམ་པར་བྱ་བའི་ཡུལ་དང་སྒོམ་པར་བྱེད་པའི་མཁན་པོ་དང་དུས་གསུམ་གྱི་སེམས་ཐམས་ཅད་ཀུང་རྒྱུད་ཐ་མི་དད་པར་ཅིར་ཡང་འཆར་གང་དུའང་མ་གྲུབ་པའི་སེམས་འདི་ཉིད་ཡིན་ལ། འདི་ཡང་ངོ་བོ་ངོས་བཟུང་བཞག་ས་རྟེན་གནས་སྐྱེ་འགག་གནས་གསུམ་དུས་གསུམ་གྱི་དབྱེ་བ་སོགས་སྒྲོ་བཏགས་ཐམས་ཅད་ཀྱིས་མ་གོས་པ།

Spend a few days looking into whether there is any difference between their identity and the identity of mind, so as to gain some decisive experience. Remind yourself by means of the previously explained pointing-out instruction of thoughts and perceptions so as to develop certainty.

Investigating the Meditation and the Meditating Mind

It isn't enough to just think that the essential meditation training is an indescribable state beyond concepts, free of arising and ceasing. Within an undistracted and wide-open state of mind, look vividly and without fixating into the identity of the meditation state. Look repeatedly to see how it is.

Likewise, look repeatedly into the meditating mind and into the mind that clings to 'I' and 'me'.

Moreover, look to see whether there is any difference between the past, future or present mind. Look into where the past mind came from, where the future mind will come from, and how the present mind is. Spend a couple of days clearing up any uncertainty you may have about this and gain a decisive experience.

The meditation object, the meditator and the mind states of past, present and future are not each of a different nature. Rather, they are this very mind that can appear in any way while not having any concrete existence whatsoever.

In its identity, mind is totally untainted by such preconceived attributes as being definable, having a location to be

གདོད་མ་ནས་གཞི་མེད་རྩལ་བྲལ་འཁྲུལ་མ་མྱོང་གྲོལ་མ་མྱོང་སྐྱོན་གྱིས་བསླད་མི་ཚུགས་ཡོན་ཏན་གྱིས་བརྒྱན་མི་ཚུགས་རང་བྱུང་རང་དག་བློ་མེད་ཟང་ཐལ་ཕྱལ་བ་ཉིད་དུ་ངོ་སྤྲོད་ལ། ཞག་འགའ་ཚེད་འཛིན་མེད་པར་རང་བབས་ལྷུག་པར་སྐྱོང་དུ་བཅུག་སྟེ་ངེས་ཤེས་ཐག་ཆོད་བསྐྱེད།

གལ་ཏེ་སླུབ་པ་པོ་བློ་རྩལ་ཞན་ན་གོང་དུ་བཤད་པའི་རྟོག་པ་དང་སྣང་བ་དང་སྒོམ་གྱི་ངོ་བོ་དང་སྒོམ་མཁན་དང་དུས་གསུམ་གྱི་ཤེས་པ་རྣམས་སོ་སོར་ཕྲལ་ལ་ཞག་མང་དུ་བལྟ་ཞིང་ཐག་ཆོད་པའི་ངེས་ཤེས་ཐོབ་ངེས་བྱ་བ་གལ་ཆེའོ།།

བཞི་པ་ནི། དེ་ནས་བསྒོམ་བྱ་སྒོམ་བྱེད་སྤྱོད་བྱ་སྤྱོད་བྱེད་རྟོགས་བྱ་རྟོགས་བྱེད་ཀྱི་བློ་རྣམས་པོར།

ཡིན་མིན་གྱི་ཡིད་བྱེད་དང་བསྒོམ་འདོད་དྲན་འདོད་སོགས་ཞེ་འདོད་ཐམས་ཅད་བཏང་།

ཅི་ཡང་ཡིད་ལ་མི་བྱེད་སྙམ་པའི་འདུན་པ་ཡང་མེད་པར་ཐ་མལ་གྱི་སེམས་བཅོས་མེད་རང་ཁ་མ་དེ་ཀར་སྤྱོད་ལུགས་ཅི་བདེ་བྱས་ལ་འདུག།

རང་ཁ་མའི་རྣམ་རྟོག་དང་སྣང་བ་ཅི་ཤར་ཡང་བློས་བཅོས་བསྒྱུར་མི་བྱ་བར་གང་དགར་བཏང་།

ཡིད་བྱེད་ཀྱི་རྗེས་སུ་ཡང་མི་འབྲང་། སེམས་དུམ་རེ་ཡེངས་པ་ལ་སྐྱོན་དུ་མི་བཟུང་ཞིང་བརྟག་དཔྱད་མི་བྱ།

placed in, a support or home, or arising, dwelling and ceasing, or distinctions of being past, present or future. From the very beginning, it is groundless and rootless, has never been subject to confusion or liberation, and is neither polluted by faults nor improved by qualities. Recognize that it is self-existing, naturally pure, unique, wide-open and pervasive. Without fixating on this being so, train for a few days in a natural and free way to gain some decisive certainty.

If the practitioner, however, is of weak intellectual power, then separate the inquiries mentioned above into the identity of thoughts, perceptions, the meditation, the meditator and the mind states of the three times. Have the practitioner look into them for quite a few days. It is essential to ensure that a decisive certainty is gained.

The Actual Transcending into Nonarising Openness

Now cast away all concerns about meditator and meditation object, experiencer and object of experience, the realizer and what is realized. Abandon all aims such as holding notions about whether or not "this is it" and the urge to meditate and be mindful. Without even the intention "I should not keep anything in mind," simply allow your ordinary mind, plain and uncontrived, to be as it naturally is.

No matter what kind of normal thought or perception habitually comes, do not try to mentally adjust or correct it; simply leave it to itself. Do not follow it up with

ནམ་དྲན་གྱི་ཚེ་བསྒོམ་རྒྱུ་སྐྱོང་རྒྱུ་བྱེད་རྒྱུ་གང་ཡང་མེད་པའི་ཐ་མལ་བཅོས་མེད་དེ་ཀར་བསྐྱུར།

ཟ་ཉལ་འཆག་གསུམ་ཡང་བློ་བྲལ་གྱི་ངང་ནས་བྱ་ཞིང་གཞན་བྱ་བ་གང་ཡང་མི་བྱ།

གཏོར་མ་དང་གསོལ་འདེབས་ཉུང་ཟད་ཙམ་རེ་མ་གཏོགས་དེ་མིན་དགེ་སྦྱོར་ཐམས་ཅད་བཞག་ལ་སླ་བ་བཅད།

ཉལ་བའི་ཚེ་ཡང་ཐ་མལ་བཅོས་མེད་ཟང་མར་ཉལ།

དེ་ལྟར་ཞག་འགའི་བར་དུ་ཡིད་བྱེད་ཐམས་ཅད་བོར་ལ་རང་ཁར་འདུག་ཏུ་བཙུག་སྟེ་ཉམས་བལྟ།

བཟང་ཞེན་གྱི་འཛིན་པ་གྲོལ་ངན་རྟོག་གི་འཁྲུལ་པ་ཟད་ནས་ཐམས་ཅད་སྒོམ་གྱི་རང་བཞིན་དུ་ངེས་ཤེས་ཐག་ཆོད་པ་སྐྱེས་ན།

ཐ་མལ་གྱི་སེམས་གང་འདུག་ཅི་ཤར་སྐྱེ་འགག་མེད་པ་སྤང་བླང་མེད་པ་བྲལ་ཐོབ་མེད་པ།

ཡིངས་མ་ཡིངས་དྲན་མ་དྲན་སྐྱོང་མ་སྐྱོང་རྟོགས་མ་རྟོགས་མེད་པར་རང་བྱུང་རང་དག་རང་གྲོལ་ཟང་ཐལ་ཐམས་ཅད་སྒོམ་གྱི་རང་བཞིན་སྒོམ་གྱི་ཁོར་ཡུག་ཏུ་ངོ་སྤྲོད་ལ་ཞག་ལྔ་ཙམ་འབྱམས་སུ་བཙུག་ཅིང་སྐབས་རེ་ཙམ་སྒོམ་མིན་པའི་སེམས་བཙལ་ཏུ་འཇུག་གོ།།

speculation. Do not regard an occasional wandering of your mind as a fault, and do not examine it.

Whenever something is thought of, let go into simply being your ordinary uncontrived state without any type of object that has to be meditated upon, savored or acted upon.

During the three activities of eating, lying down or moving about, do them within a state of being free from concepts, and refrain from any other activity. Apart from a small amount of torma offering and supplication, set aside all other types of spiritual practice and remain silent. When lying down, do so in an ordinary, uncontrived and open state.

In this way, for a couple of days, cast all kinds of mental doing aside and remain as you naturally are, and thus gain some experience.

At some point, the clinging to good dissolves, the confusion of negative thought wears out and you gain the definite assurance that everything is the very substance of the training. Ordinary mind — exactly as it is and during any type of experience — should then be pointed out as neither arising nor ceasing, neither to be accepted nor rejected, neither to be without nor achieved. It should be pointed out as being a self-existing natural purity, a self-liberated openness that is neither distracted nor undistracted, neither remembered nor forgotten, neither experienced nor not experienced, neither realized nor unrealized. Everything is the substance of the training and everything is uninterrupted training. Be suspended like this for about

ལྔ་པ་ནི། དེ་ལྟར་སྒོམ་འཁོར་ཡུག་དེས་མཉམ་གཞག་དང་རྗེས་ཐོབ་བསྲེ་ཞིང༌། རྗེས་ཐོབ་ཏུ་དུམ་རེ་ཡེངས་ན་ཡང་རྗེས་ཤེས་དྲན་པས་ནམ་ཟིན་གནས་ལུགས་དེ་རིག་པས་ཆོག།

དེ་བཞིན་དུ་ཉིན་མོའི་ཁོར་ཡུག་དེ་མཚན་མོར་བསྲེ་ཞིང་གཉིད་དང་རྨི་ལམ་དུ་བསྐྱངས་ན་མཆོག་ཡིན།

དེ་མིན་འཁྲུལ་ཡང་སད་མ་ཐག་རྗེས་ལ་གནས་ལུགས་རིག་པས་ཆོག།

གཞན་མཚན་བཅས་དང་ཡིད་བྱེད་གང་ཡང་མི་བྱ་བར་ཞག་ལྔ་རེ་ཙམ་བཞག། ཡང་ཞག་རེ་ཙམ་གང་བདེར་ངལ་གསོ།

ཡང་ཞག་བདུན་རེ་བཅུ་རེ་ཙམ་དུ་ལ་བཟླ་རེ་དང་ངལ་གསོ་རེ་སྤེལ་ལ་གནས་ལུགས་ཀྱི་རྟོགས་པ་དེས་ཉིན་པར་ཁོར་ཡུག་ཏུ་མ་སོང་བར་དུ་ལ་བཟླ།

ཉིན་པར་ཁོར་ཡུག་ཏུ་སོང་ནས་མཚན་མོ་རིམ་གྱིས་འཆར་བ་ཡིན་ནོ།།

ལ་བཟླ་འདི་ལ་སྒོམ་ཁོར་ཡུག་གི་མན་ངག་ཀྱང་ཟེར།

མཉམ་མེད་དྭགས་པོའི་གབ་པ་མངོན་ཕྱུང་གི་དགོངས་པ་གནས་ལུགས་རྗེན་པ་གཏན་ལ་དབབ་པའི་བོགས་འདོན་ཡིན་པས་མན་ངག་འདི་གནད་འཚམས་ཟློས་ན། གཉུག་མ་བཟང་ཞེན་ཅན་གྱིས་ལོ་མང་དུ་བགྲོད་དགོས་པའི་རྟོགས་པ་ཞག་འགའ་ལ་བགྲོད་ནུས་པ་ཡིན་ནོ།།

five days and only occasionally try to seek a state of mind that is not meditation training.

Mingling Meditation and Postmeditation, Day and Night

This type of uninterrupted training mingles the composure and the postmeditation. When there is an occasional distraction during the postmeditation, it is enough simply to recognize the natural state, whenever it is remembered, with the mindfulness of the ensuing understanding.

Likewise, it is most eminent when the constancy of the daytime mingles into night to embrace both the sleep and dream states. If that is not the case and you become deluded, it is nevertheless sufficient to recognize the natural state immediately upon waking up.

Remain like this for about five days without any other type of conceptual practice and without any mental doing whatsoever.

After that, take rest for a few days in whichever way you please. Next, spend seven to ten days on transcendence, alternating it with rest. Thus transcend until your realization of the natural state is uninterrupted throughout the day. Once it has become constant during the daytime it will gradually be experienced during the night.

This way of transcending is also known as the *instruction in constant training*. It is the intent of the incomparable Gampopa's *Revealing the Hidden*[15] to bring forth enhancement in establishing the naked, natural state. For this reason, if you follow this instruction precisely, in a

ཅི་ཀྱང་བོགས་མ་ཐོན་ན་རེ་ཞིག་མཉམ་རྗེས་ཀྱི་དགེ་སྦྱོར་སྐྱོང་ལུགས་སྔར་བཞིན་བྱའོ།

༈ ལྔ་པ་ལམ་ཁྱེར་སྤྱོད་པའི་སྒོ་ནས་རྒྱལ་སྦྱོང་བ་ལ་བདུན།

ལམ་ཁྱེར་གྱི་དུས་དང་སྤྱོད་པ།

རྣམ་རྟོག་ལམ་ཁྱེར།

ཉོན་མོངས་ལམ་ཁྱེར།

ལྷ་འདྲེ་ལམ་ཁྱེར།

སྡུག་བསྔལ་ལམ་ཁྱེར།

ན་ཚ་ལམ་ཁྱེར།

འཆི་བ་ལམ་ཁྱེར་རོ།།

དང་པོ་ནི། སྒོམ་ངོ་མཐོང་གི་རྟོགས་པ་ཤར་ནས་ཚེ་འདིའི་སྣང་ཤས་ལ་སོང་བ་དང་རྐྱེན་དྲག་པོ་དང་འཕྲད་པ་དང་རྣམ་རྟོག་བག་ལ་ཉལ་ངོ་མ་ཤེས་འོང་བའི་དུས་དང་། མདོར་ན་དགེ་སྦྱོར་གྱི་རང་ཤུགས་སུ་ལམ་དུ་སློང་དཀའ་བའི་འཁྲུ་འཕྲིག་གི་འཛིན་པ་ནམ་བྱུང་གི་དུས་དང་།

དབེན་པའི་གནས་སུ་སྒོམ་ཁོར་ཡུག་ཤར་ན་དེ་བརྟན་ཞིང་བོགས་དབྱུང་བ་ལ་སྤྱོད་པ་བྱ་བའི་ཚོ་གོང་གི་རྐྱེན་དང་འཁྲུ་འཕྲིག་བྱུང་བའི་དུས་རྣམས་སུ་ལམ་ཁྱེར་བྱ་སྟེ།

matter of days you can cover a realization that otherwise would take many years while clinging to something pleasant as being the natural state.

If this enhancement is not reached, then for a while the way of continuing the spiritual practices of the composure and postmeditation should be carried out as before.

Developing Strength by Utilizing the Conducts

This has seven points:

The time for the utilizing and the conducts
Utilizing thoughts
Utilizing emotions
Utilizing gods and demons
Utilizing suffering
Utilizing sickness
Utilizing the process of dying

The Time for Utilizing and the Conducts

After you have had the realization of recognizing the meditation state, the time for utilizing is when you eagerly hanker after the things of this life, when you meet with severe difficulties or when there are latent thoughts the nature of which you do not recognize. In short, it is meant for whenever you entertain a worried type of clinging that makes it hard to continue your spiritual practice naturally.

Utilizing is also for being in retreat, when your meditation training has become steadfast. Apply it to stabilize

གཞན་དུ་ན་སྣང་སྲིད་ལམ་ཁྱེར་གྱི་རྒྱལ་པོ་བློ་བྲལ་གནས་ལུགས་སྐྱོང་བ་དོར་ནས་གཉེན་པོ་ཅན་གྱི་ལམ་ཁྱེར་བསྒོམ་པ་དོན་མིན་ནོ།།

དེ་ལ་སྤྱོད་པ་བྱ་བའི་དུས་ནི་མཉམ་རྗེས་ཁོར་ཡུག་ཏུ་གྱུར་ནས་བྱ་ལ། སྤྱོད་པ་ནི་གསང་སྔགས་ཀྱི་ལམ་ནས་སྤྲོས་བཅས་སྤྲོས་མེད་ཤིན་ཏུ་སྤྲོས་མེད་གསུམ་མམ། ཀུན་ཏུ་བཟང་པོའི་སྤྱོད་པ་གསང་སྤྱོད་རིག་པ་བརྟུལ་ཞུགས་ཀྱི་སྤྱོད་པ་ཚོགས་སྤྱོད་ཕྱོགས་ལས་རྣམ་རྒྱལ་གྱི་སྤྱོད་པ་སོགས་མང་དུ་གསུངས་ཀྱང་།

འདིར་སྒོམ་པོགས་འདོན་གྱི་སྤྱོད་པ་ལ་རབ་བྱུང་གི་བསླབ་པ་དང་མི་འགལ་བར་ཀུན་བཟང་དང་། སྤྲོས་མེད་དང་ཤིན་ཏུ་སྤྲོས་མེད་དང་ཕྱོགས་ལས་རྣམ་རྒྱལ་གྱི་སྤྱོད་པ་དང་དོན་མཐུན་པར། རི་བོའི་རྩེ་དང་གཉན་ས་དང་དུར་ཁྲོད་དང་ཤིང་གཅིག་གི་མདུན་དང་བཞི་མདོ་ལ་སོགས་པའི་གནས་རྣམས་སུ་སླ་བ་བཅད་དེ་ཀུ་སུ་ལུའི་མཆོད་སྦྱིན་བྱ་ཞིང་།

འཇིག་རྟེན་ལ་བློ་མི་འཇུག་པ་རི་དྭགས་རྨྲས་མ་ལྟ་བུའི་སྤྱོད་པ།

ཅི་བྱུང་ཡང་ཉམ་ང་མེད་པ་སེངྒེ་ལྟ་བུའི་སྤྱོད་པ། གང་ལ་ཡང་ཆགས་ཞེན་མེད་པ་བར་སྣང་གི་རླུང་ལྟ་བུའི་སྤྱོད་པ། ཅི་ལའང་བློ་རྟེན་མི་བཅའ་བ་ནམ་མཁའ་ལྟ་བུའི་སྤྱོད་པ། དགག་སྒྲུབ་དང་གཟའ་གཏད་མེད་པ་སྨྱོན་པ་ལྟ་བུའི་སྤྱོད་པ་སྟེ་ལྔའི་སྒོ་ནས་རྒྱེན་མཐའ་དག་ལམ་དུ་སློང་ཞིང་གནས་ལུགས་ལ་པོགས་དབྱུང་བར་བྱའོ།།

and enhance your practice when you engage in the various types of conduct and when you encounter the difficulties and worries mentioned above.

Apart from this, there is no point in casting aside the king-like practice of utilizing all that appears and exists by sustaining the natural state free of conceptual attitude in order to train in another form of remedy-oriented practice. The time for utilizing is when your meditation and postmeditation have become steadfast.

The types of conduct to utilize are the three types of elaborate, unelaborate and extremely unelaborate conduct belonging to the path of Secret Mantra — or, the ever-excellent conduct, the secret conduct, the awareness conduct of yogic discipline, the group conduct, the conduct of complete victory and so forth.

Many such types have been taught, but in this case, as a conduct for enhancing the meditation training, apply the ever-excellent conduct that is not in conflict with the monastic trainings. As well, in agreement with the unelaborate, very unelaborate and the conduct of complete victory, go to such places as a mountain top, a haunted place, a charnel ground, under a large tree or at a crossroad and make the *kusulu* offering and giving while avoiding conversation.[16] Also, make use of one of these five types: the wounded deer conduct of being uninvolved in the world, the lion-like conduct of being unafraid of whatever happens, the wind-like conduct of not being attached to anything, the space-like conduct of not relying on anything whatsoever, or the madman conduct of being

གཉིས་པ་ནི། དགེ་མི་དགེ་ལ་སོགས་པའི་རྣམ་པར་རྟོག་པ་ཤར་ནས་ལྷུ་འཕྲིག་བྱུང་བའི་ཚེ། རྣམ་རྟོག་དེ་ངོས་བཟུང་ནས་གང་ཤར་དེ་མ་བཅོས་ལྷུག་པར་སྐྱོང་སྟེ། དེ་ཡང་རྟོག་པ་དེ་ཡིད་ལ་མི་བྱེད་པར་སེམས་བཀུག་ནས་གཉེན་པོ་ཡེ་ཤེས་བསྒོམ་པ་ཡང་མིན།

རྟོག་པ་དེའི་ངོ་བོ་ལ་བརྟག་དཔྱད་བྱས་ཏེ་རང་བཞིན་མ་གྲུབ་པར་གཏན་ལ་འབེབས་པ་ཡང་མིན།

རྟོག་པ་དེའི་རྗེས་སུ་འབྲང་ཞིང་དྲན་པས་སྐྱོང་བ་ཡང་མིན་པར།

རྟོག་པ་དེ་ངོ་ཤེས་ཙམ་ནས་རྟོག་པ་དེ་ཀ་ལ་སྒོམ་གྱི་ངོ་བོར་བྱས་ཏེ་ཅི་ལྟར་འདུག་པ་དེ་ལ་སྐྱོན་དུ་མི་བཟུང་ཆེད་དུ་མི་དགག་རྗེས་སུའང་མི་འབྲང་བར་དེ་ག་ལ་བློས་མ་བཅོས་པར་གསལ་ལེ་ཡེ་རེ་ལྷོད་དེ་གུ་ཡངས་སང་ངེ་བཞག་པས།

རྟོག་པ་གང་ཤར་དེ་ཉིད་སྤང་བླང་དགག་སྒྲུབ་བཅོས་བསྒྱུར་མི་དགོས་པར་སྒོམ་དུ་ལྷངས་ཀྱིས་འཆར་ཏེ། དེ་ལ་རྣམ་རྟོག་ལམ་དུ་སློང་བ་ཞེས་བྱའོ།།

གློང་དུ་མ་གྱུར་པས་རྣམ་རྟོག་གི་གཡོ་བ་དྲག་པོ་རྣམས་དང་པོར་མི་བདེ་ཁར་རེ་བ་འདྲ་བ་ཞིག་དང་དམ་ཤུགས་ཀྱིས་ལམ་དུ་ལོངས་ལ།

རིམ་གྱིས་གློང་དུ་གྱུར་ནས་མཐར་ངོས་ཟིན་པ་ཙམ་གྱིས་ལམ་དུ་བསླང་བ་ཡིན་ནོ།།

free from judgment and reference point. By means of these five types, utilize every difficult situation to enhance the natural state.

Utilizing Thoughts

When you begin to worry about various good and evil thoughts arising, recognize the thought and sustain unfabricated naturalness in whatever arises. This does not mean that you should concentrate in an attempt not to think the thought while using original wakefulness as its remedy. It also does not mean that you should try to analyze the thought's identity to establish its lack of a real nature. Nor does it mean that you should try to pursue the thought while maintaining mindfulness.

What it means is this: recognize the thought's nature and simply make that the essence of your meditation training. No matter how it is, do not regard the thought as a fault. Do not deliberately try to suppress it. Do not get involved in it. Rather, without trying to change it, simply suspend it, in a way that is naked and clear, relaxed, spacious and free.

In this way, the arising of any thought does not need to be confirmed or denied, accepted or rejected, adjusted or corrected, but vividly becomes the meditation training itself. This is known as *utilizing thoughts*.

Because of not having mastered this principle, turbulent movements of thought seem at first frightfully problematic. Now, plunge straight into utilizing them. Gradu-

གསུམ་པ་ནི། ཉོན་མོངས་པ་འདོད་ཆགས་ཞེ་སྡང་གཏི་མུག་ང་རྒྱལ་ཕྲག་དོག་ལྟ་གང་ཡང་རུང་བ་སྐྱེས་པའི་ཚེ་དེ་ངོས་བཟུང་སྟེ་དེ་དགག་ཀྱང་མི་དགག་རྗེས་སུ་ཡང་མི་འབྲང་བར་ཉོན་མོངས་པ་དེ་ཀ་བློས་མ་བཅོས་པར་གསལ་སིང་ངེ་བར་གུ་ཡངས་སང་ངེ་བཞག་པས་སྒོམ་དུ་འཆར་རོ།།

སྐབས་རེ་ཉོན་མོངས་པའི་དམིགས་རྐྱེན་ཕྱི་རྫས་ནང་སེམས་ཅན་གང་ཡིན་པའི་ཆགས་ཡུལ་སྡང་ཡུལ་ལ་སོགས་སྔར་ལས་མངོན་ཚན་ཆེ་བ་ཡིད་ལ་བྱས་ཏེ་ཉོན་མོངས་པ་ཆེས་ཆེར་བསྐྱེད་ལ། སྐྱེས་པ་དང་སྔར་བཞིན་བསྐྱང་ངོ།།

གཏི་མུག་ལ་གཉིད་བྲོ་བའི་སེམས་དེ་ངོས་བཟུང་ལ་གཉིད་ཐིབས་ཐིབས་ཡོང་བའི་ཚེ་དེ་ཀའི་སྟེང་དུ་བློས་མ་བཅོས་པར་བསྐྱང་བས་གཉིད་འོད་གསལ་དུ་འཆར་བའི་ཐབས་སུ་འགྱུར་ཞིང་། གློང་དུ་གྱུར་མ་གྱུར་སྔར་ལྟར་འབྱུང་ངོ།།

བཞི་པ་ནི། ལྷ་འདྲེའི་ཚོ་འཕྲུལ་ལ་སོགས་པས་འཇིགས་ཤིང་བག་ཚ་ཟིང་སྟེ་བྱུང་བའི་ཚེ། འཇིགས་པའི་རྟོག་པ་ངོས་བཟུང་ལ་མི་དགག་རྗེས་མི་འབྲང་བར་འཇིགས་རྟོག་དེ་ཀ་བློས་མ་བཅོས་པར་གསལ་རྗེན་ལྷང་ངེ་བསྐྱངས་པས་སྒོམ་དུ་འཆར། ཚོ་འཕྲུལ་སླ་དབབ་ན་དེ་ལས་འཇིགས་པའི་ཚོ་འཕྲུལ་བློར་མི་ཤོང་བ་བྱུང་བར་བསམས་ཏེ་འཇིགས་སྣང་ཡང་ཆེར་བསྐྱེད་ལ་གོང་བཞིན་ཉམས་སུ་བླང་ངོ།།

ally you will master them, so that eventually they become utilized the very moment you recognize them.

Utilizing Emotions

When you feel an emotion such as any of the five types — attachment, anger, dullness pride or envy — simply recognize it. Do not attempt to suppress it. Do not indulge in it. Do not mentally try to alter it. Instead, suspend the emotion itself, in a way that is lucidly present and with a spacious openness.

From time to time try to create a more intense emotion by bringing to mind something even more provocative than the previous objects, such as the objects of attachment or anger, whatever they may be — outer material things or sentient beings. Once the emotion is created, continue the practice as before.

Concerning dullness, recognize the attitude of dozing off into sleep. When about to drop off, without trying to mentally alter it, sustain the state of simply being in that. This will become a way to let sleep dawn as luminosity. Continue as above until this is mastered.

Utilizing Gods and Demons

When full of dread and terror caused by magical displays of gods and demons or the like, recognize the fearful thought. Neither suppress nor indulge it. Rather than trying to correct it, train in simply being in that fearful

ལྔ་པ་ནི། སྤྱིར་འཁོར་བར་སྡུག་བསྔལ་བ་དང་ཁྱད་པར་ཡུལ་སེམས་ཅན་ཞིག་སྡུག་བསྔལ་བ་མཐོང་ན། དེ་ལ་སྙིང་རྗེ་མེད་པར་རང་དེ་འདྲར་གྱུར་དོགས་ནས་སྒོམ་ལ་སེམས་སྦྱོ་བ་ཐེག་དམན་གྱི་བློ་དང་།

དེ་ལ་སྙིང་བརྩེ་སྐྱེས་ཤིང་དེས་མཚོན་པའི་སེམས་ཅན་ཐམས་ཅད་ལ་སྙིང་བརྩེ་སྐྱེ་བ་ཐེག་ཆེན་གྱི་བློ་གང་སྐྱེས་ཀྱང་།

བློ་དེ་ངོས་བཟུང་ལ་དེ་ལ་བློས་མ་བཅོས་པར་གསལ་ལྷང་ངེ་བཞག་ལ་ལམ་དུ་སློང་ཉམས་དེའི་ངང་མ་ཤོར་བར་སེམས་ཅན་ཀུན་ལ་བྱམས་སྙིང་རྗེ་བྱང་ཆུབ་ཀྱི་སེམས་བསྐྱེད་དེ་སྨོན་ལམ་གདབ་བོ།།

དྲུག་པ་ནི། རང་ནད་ཀྱི་རིགས་གང་ཡང་རུང་བས་ན་བའི་ཚེ་རྒྱུ་རྐྱེན་སོགས་ཀྱི་བརྟག་དཔྱད་མི་བསམ་ཞིང་དགག་སྒྲུབ་མ་ཤོར་བར་བྱས་ཏེ།

ན་ཚ་ཟུག་གཟེར་ལྷང་ངེ་བ་དེ་ཉིད་སྒོམ་གྱི་ངོ་བོར་བྱས་ལ་བློས་མ་བཅོས་པར་གསལ་སིང་ངེ་བཞག།

དེ་ཡུན་བསྲིངས་པས་ན་ཚ་སྦྱོང་མི་དགོས་པར་སྒོམ་དུ་འཆར་ཞིང་བོགས་ཐོན་ནོ།།

ནད་སྒྲ་དབབ་ན་སྔར་དང་འདྲ།

thought in a way that is clear, naked and awake. By doing so the thought is experienced as the meditation training.

If the magical displays subside, imagine that an even more terrifying and mind-boggling magical display unfolds. Increase the fear even further and continue the practice as before.

Utilizing Suffering

When seeing, in general, that samsara is painful or, in particular, a sentient being who is suffering, rather than feeling compassion the Hinayana attitude is to be inspired to practice out of fear that oneself may suffer. The Mahayana attitude is to feel both loving kindness and love for that one being and, exemplified thereby, for all sentient beings.

Whichever is the case, utilize that particular attitude by recognizing it and, without trying to mentally alter it, suspend it in a lucid state of being awake.

While not losing the continuity of that experience, generate loving kindness, compassion and bodhichitta for all sentient beings, and make aspirations.

Utilizing Sickness

When sick from a disease, do not worry about its particular causes, circumstances, etc. Do not get involved in suppressing or encouraging it. Use the acute feeling of ache and pain as the very substance of the training and,

གཞན་ཡང་ན་མཁན་གཟེར་མཁན་སྨྱོང་མཁན་གྱི་བདག་འཛིན་རྩད་གཅོད་པ་དང་ངོ་བོ་ངོས་བཟུང་མེད་པའི་ངང་ལ་མ་བཅོས་པར་འཛོག་པ་སོགས་ཀྱང་བྱའོ།།

འདིར་རོ་སྙོམས་པས་སྨན་དཔྱད་སྤང་བར་བཞེད་ཀྱང་རང་གི་ནད་དགེ་སྦྱོར་དུ་འཁྱེར་བ་ཡིན་གྱི།

བྱང་ཆུབ་སྒྲུབ་པའི་རྟེན་ལ་ཤི་མ་ཤི་མེད་པར་སྨན་འཚོས་མི་བྱའོ།།

བདུན་པ་ནི། དེ་ལྟར་མི་ཚེ་གང་བྱུང་ལ་རྐྱེན་ཅི་བྱུང་ལམ་དུ་འཁྱེར་ནས་གོམས་པར་བྱས་ལ།

འཆི་བའི་ཚེ་ཐིམ་རིམ་རིམ་ཅན་ལ་སོགས་པ་ཅི་ཤར་ཡང་ངོ་ཤེས་པ་ཙམ་བྱས་ལ་རེ་དོགས་དང་དགག་སྒྲུབ་ཀྱི་ཡུ་འཕྲིག་མི་བྱ་བར་གང་ཤར་ཤར་དེ་ཀ་ལ་བློས་མ་བཅོས་པར་གསལ་རྗེན་ལྷང་ངེ་བསྐྱངས་པས།

ཐིམ་རིམ་རྫོགས་པའི་རྗེས་ལ་རང་བཞིན་གྱི་འོད་གསལ་འཆར་བ་དང་ལམ་དུ་བསྐྱངས་པའི་འོད་གསལ་དེ་མ་བུ་འདྲེས་པས་ཆུ་ལ་ཆུ་བཞག་པའམ་ནམ་མཁའ་དང་ནམ་མཁའ་འདྲེས་པ་ལྟར་གྱུར་ཏེ་སངས་རྒྱ་བར་བཤད་ཅིང་།

གལ་ཏེ་གོམས་པ་ཆུང་བས་སངས་མ་རྒྱས་ཀྱང་བར་དོ་དང་སྐྱེ་བའི་ལམ་ཁྱེར་སྐོར་གྱི་ཤུགས་ཀྱིས་རང་དབང་ཐོབ་པར་བཤད་དོ།།

without trying to alter it, suspend it in being vividly present.

By continuing in this way, you find progress in that the pain becomes the meditation training without having to be rejected. If the sickness subsides, practice as mentioned above.[17]

Moreover, investigate the ego-clinging within the one who feels sick, the one who hurts and the one who experiences, and suspend it without artifice in the state that is free from any definable identity.

Practitioners of Equal Taste, *Ro-Nyom*, may hold that one should now give up medical treatment. Here, in this context, it is more a matter of using your sickness for spiritual training, rather than foolishly assuming that it does not matter whether or not the physical support for attaining enlightenment dies.

Utilizing the Process of Dying

In this way one should train by utilizing whatever happens and whatever circumstance is encountered. When the time of death arrives, no matter what takes place, including the gradual sequence of dissolution stages and so forth, simply recognize them. Do not get involved in the worry of hope or fear, of suppressing or encouraging. Instead, sustain the practice in a lucid state of naked wakefulness, in exactly whatever it is that unfolds, without trying to correct it.

At the end, after the dissolution stages have finished, it is taught that mother and child intermingle — the dawn

ལམ་ཁྱེར་འདི་དག་མཉམ་མེད་དྭགས་པོའི་གསུང་རབ་ལས་འཕོར་བུར་གསུངས་ཤིང་རྐྱེན་སྣང་ཅི་བྱུང་ཅི་ཤར་ཕྱག་རྒྱ་ཆེན་པོར་འཁྱེར་ནས་རོ་སྙོམས་པ་ལ་དོན་ཚང་ཡང་།

ཕྱིས་སྒྲུབ་བརྒྱུད་པ་རྣམས་ཀྱིས་ལམ་ཁྱེར་དྲུག་དམིགས་བསལ་དུ་ཕྱེ་བ་རྒྱལ་སྤྱོད་དུ་ལེགས་པ་འདུག་ཅིང་བློ་རིགས་ཕལ་ཆེར་ལ་ཁྱད་ཆེ་བར་སྣང་བས་དེ་ལྟར་དུ་བྱས་པ་སྟེ་མིང་གཞན་རོ་སྙོམས་ཞེས་ཀྱང་གྲགས་སོ།།

དྲུག་པ་རྟོགས་པ་འཆར་ཚུལ་བོགས་འདོན་དང་བཅས་པ་ལ་ལྔ།

འཆར་ཚུལ་མི་འདྲ་བའི་ཁྱད་པར།

རྩེ་གཅིག་བོགས་འདོན་དང་བཅས་པ།

སྤྲོས་བྲལ་བོགས་འདོན་དང་བཅས་པ།

རོ་གཅིག་བོགས་འདོན་དང་བཅས་པ།

སྒོམ་མེད་བོགས་འདོན་དང་བཅས་པའོ།།

དང་པོ་ནི། གང་ཟག་ཅིག་ཆར་བའི་རིགས་ལ་དང་པོར་གནས་པའི་དུས་སམ་ངོ་སྤྲོད་དུས་ནས་རྩེ་གཅིག་ཙམ་དང་སྤྲོས་བྲལ་མན་དང་རོ་གཅིག་མན་དང་སྒོམ་མེད་ཕྱིན་ཅིག་ཆར་དུ་སྐྱེ་བ་སོགས་སྣ་ཚོགས་པ་ཡོད་ལ་སྐྱེས་པ་དེ་ཡང་བརྟན་ནོ།།

of the *natural luminosity* and the *path luminosity* you have trained in — and that through this you awaken to enlightenment, like water poured into water or like space mingling with space.

If, on the other hand, you do not awaken because your familiarity is weak, it is taught that through your former training in utilizing you can attain mastery in the bardo or in your next rebirth.

These ways of utilizing are found in the various writings of the incomparable Gampopa. The main principle is contained in utilizing whatever happens in any situation as being Mahamudra and so equalizing its 'taste'. The masters of the Practice Lineage in the following ages, however, specified six ways of utilizing, and so we have these excellent trainings. Their aptness seems to vary for different types of people and should therefore be used accordingly. Under another name, they are known as Equal Taste.

How Realization Arises and the Enhancement Practices

This has five points:

The various ways realization arises
One-pointedness and its enhancement
Simplicity and its enhancement
One Taste and its enhancement
Nonmeditation and its enhancement

ཐོད་རྒལ་བ་ལ་རྣལ་འབྱོར་བཞི་སྔ་མ་མ་བརྟན་པར་ཕྱི་མ་ཐོལ་གྱིས་སྐྱེ་ལ་སྐྱེས་པ་མི་བརྟན་པར་འཕེལ་འགྲིབ་ཆེ་བས་མཚམས་ལ་རྒྱུན་དུ་གནས་ཤིང་རྩེ་གཅིག་ཏུ་བསྒོམས་ན་རྟོགས་པ་བརྟན་པོ་ཐོབ་ལ། ཚེ་འདིར་སྒོམ་ཡུན་ཐུང་ན་རྟོགས་པ་གཤའ་མ་བར་དོར་འཆར་བར་བཤད་དོ།།

རིམ་གྱིས་པ་ལ་རྣལ་འབྱོར་བཞི་རིམ་པས་འཆར་ཞིང་སྔ་མ་བརྟན་ནས་ཕྱི་མ་རིམ་གྱིས་སྐྱེ་ལ་སྐྱེས་པ་ཡང་བརྟན་ཏེ་སྙིང་རུས་བསྐྱེད་པ་གལ་ཆེའོ།།

ཐོད་རྒལ་བ་དང་རིམ་གྱིས་པ་གཉིས་ཀྱང་བླ་མ་ལ་མོས་གུས་དང་སྒོམ་ལ་སྙིང་རུས་བསྐྱེད་ན་ཅིག་ཆར་བ་དང་འདྲ་བར་འགྱུར་བ་ལ་ཚོགས་མེད་པར་བཤད་ཅིང་།

རིགས་གསུམ་པོ་སོ་སོ་ལའང་བློ་རྩལ་ཆེ་ཆུང་གི་དབྱེ་བས་སྐྱེ་ལུགས་མ་ངེས་པ་སྣ་ཚོགས་འོང་བར་འདུག་པས། རྣལ་འབྱོར་བཞི་རིམ་གྱི་བཤད་ཚོད་ཐམས་ཅད་ཁྲིགས་ཀྱིས་འགྲིགས་པ་རང་གི་ངེས་བཟུང་མི་སྣང་ལ།

འོན་ཀྱང་རིམ་གྱིས་པ་ལ་རིམ་ཅན་ངེས་བཟུང་དུ་འཆར་བའི་ཚུལ་བཤད་ན་མ་ངེས་པའི་འཆར་ཚུལ་ལའང་དགེ་སྦྱོར་གྱི་གནས་སྐབས་དང་བླང་དོར་ཕྱེད་པས་དེ་ལྟར་དུ་བཤད་པར་བྱའོ།།

The Various Ways Realization Arises

For the person of the instantaneous type, from the very onset of stillness, from One-Pointedness after being pointed out, from Simplicity or from One Taste, the progress up to Nonmeditation can take place at once, etc., and this progress is stable.

For the person of the skipping-the-grades type, the next of the four yogas happens suddenly before the previous is stabilized, and this progress is unstable and will fluctuate considerably. If such a person remains continuously in retreat and trains one-pointedly, he will attain stability. If his period of practice during this life is but a short while, it is taught that he will have true realization in the bardo.

For the person of the gradual type, the four yogas occur in a sequence in that the following happens gradually after the previous has been stabilized, and this occurrence is steadfast. So it essential to persevere.

It is taught that when people of both the skipping-the-grades type and the gradual type train in guru devotion and are resolute, they will have no great difficulty in being like the instantaneous type.

There is a range of variables for how these yogas occur since each of the three types of people can be divided according to their degree of mental aptitude. So it doesn't seem possible to systematize an exact description of the sequence of the four yogas. Nevertheless, here I shall explain the clear-cut progressive order for the gradual type of person, since it includes both the spiritual practices as well

བཞིས་པ་ནི། རྩེ་གཅིག་གི་རྣལ་འབྱོར་ལ་གོམས་པ་ཆུང་འབྲིང་ཆེ་གསུམ་གྱི་དབྱེ་བས་གསུམ་དུ་ཡོད་དེ།

གསལ་སྟོང་བདེ་ཉམས་དང་བཅས་པའི་ཏིང་ངེ་འཛིན་སྐྱོང་དཀའ་བ་ཙམ་ནས་ནམ་སྒོམ་སྒོམ་འོང་བའི་བར་རྩེ་གཅིག་ཆུང་ངུ།

རེས་མ་བསྒོམས་ཀྱང་ཏིང་ངེ་འཛིན་དེ་ར་འགྲོ་ཞིང་བསྒོམས་པའི་ཚེ་བརྟན་པོ་འོང་བ་རྩེ་གཅིག་འབྲིང་།

མཉམ་རྗེས་དང་སྤྱོད་ལམ་བཞི་དང་ཉིན་མཚན་ཁོར་ཡུག་ཏུ་རྒྱུན་ཆད་མེད་པར་གསལ་སྟོང་གི་ངང་དུ་ཆམ་གྱིས་འགྲོ་བ་རྩེ་གཅིག་ཆེན་པོའོ།།

དེ་ཡང་མཐར་ཕྱིན་མ་ཕྱིན་དབྱེ་བ་དྲུག་གིས་བྱེད་དེ།

སེམས་གསལ་སྟོང་དེ་ཉིད་ལ་རང་རིག་ཡིད་ཆེས་ཀྱི་ངེས་ཤེས་སྐྱེད་ན་རྩེ་གཅིག་གི་ངོ་བོ་མཐོང་།

བདེ་གསལ་མི་རྟོག་པའི་ངང་དུ་གནས་ཀྱང་ངེས་ཤེས་ཀྱི་འཕྲིག་མ་ཚུད་ན་ངོ་བོ་མ་མཐོང་།

གསལ་སྟོང་དེའི་ངང་ལ་ཉིན་མཚན་ཁོར་ཡུག་ཏུ་འགྲོ་ན་རྩལ་རྫོགས།

རེས་འཇོག་འོང་ན་རྩལ་མ་རྫོགས།

as the points to be accepted and rejected that pertain to the indefinite ways realization arises.

One-Pointedness and Its Enhancement

For the yoga of One-Pointedness, there are three stages due to the difference in higher, medium and lesser degrees of proficiency.

The lesser One-Pointedness is from the time when the samadhi of aware emptiness endowed with the bliss experience is somewhat difficult to maintain up to when the meditation state happens whenever you train.

The medium One-Pointedness is when, from time to time, you arrive in samadhi even without practicing, and when practicing it becomes stable.

The higher One-Pointedness is when you totally arrive in the state of aware emptiness — unceasingly during the meditation state and postmeditation, the four daily activities and throughout day and night.

❧

Furthermore, there are these six distinctions as to whether or not perfection has been reached:

You have seen the essence of One-Pointedness if you have reached a naturally knowing and confident certainty in your mind's aware emptiness. You have not seen the essence if you do not possess this confident certitude, even if you can remain in the states of bliss, clarity and non-thought.

རྟོག་སྣང་ཤར་ཚད་དྲན་པས་ཟིན་ཙམ་ནས་སྤྱང་མ་དགོས་པར་སྒོམ་དུ་འགྲོ་ན་རྣམ་རྟོག་སྒོམ་དུ་ཤར།

རྣམ་རྟོག་བཀུག་ནས་བསྒོམ་དགོས་ན་མ་ཤར།

ཆོས་བརྒྱད་ལས་བློ་ལོག་པ་སོགས་ཀྱི་དྲོད་རྟགས་ཐོབ་ན་ཡོན་ཏན་སྐྱེས། བློ་ལས་སུ་མི་རུང་བ་སོགས་འདུག་ན་མ་སྐྱེས།

རྗེས་ཤེས་སུ་སེམས་ཅན་ལ་སྙིང་རྗེ་སྐྱེ་ཞིང་གཞན་ཕན་གྱི་སྨོན་ལམ་བཏབ་ན་གཟུགས་སྐུའི་ས་བོན་ཐེབས།

སྙིང་རྗེ་སྐྱེ་དཀའ་ན་མ་ཐེབས། རྗེས་ཤེས་སུ་རྒྱུ་འབྲས་ཕྲ་རགས་ལ་མི་སླུ་བའི་འཕྲིག་ཚུད་ན་ཀུན་རྫོབ་ལ་རང་བྱིན་ཚུད།

རྒྱུ་འབྲས་ཀྱི་རྟེན་འབྲེལ་ལ་ངེས་པ་མ་རྙེད་ན་མ་ཚུད་པའོ།།

དེ་ལ་རྩེ་གཅིག་ཆུང་ངུའི་དུས། སེམས་གསལ་སྟོང་བདེ་ཉམས་དང་བཅས་པའི་མཉམ་བཞག་ངེས་བཟུང་ཅན་ཡོད་ཅིང་ཉམས་དེའི་ངང་ནས་རྟོག་སྣང་འཆར་བའི་ཚེ་རང་དྭངས་རང་གྲོལ་དུ་འགྲོ་ཞིང་སྒོམ་ཡིན་སྙམ་དུ་བློས་བྱས་ཀྱི་ངེས་ཤེས་ཀྱང་འོང་། རྗེས་སྣང་དུ་དགའ་སྤྲོ་དང་བཅས་པའི་སྣང་བ་ཕལ་ཆེར་ཨ་འཐས་སུ་འཆར།

རྗེས་ཤེས་སུ་དྲན་པས་ནམ་ཟིན་གསལ་སྟོང་གི་ཉམས་དང་བཅས་ཏེ་སྟོང་པ་དང་སེམས་སྣང་ཡིན་སྙམ་པའི་འཛིན་སྟངས་འབྱུང་།

You have perfected the strength of One-Pointedness if this state of aware emptiness becomes constant throughout day and night. You have not perfected its strength if it is an occasional resting.

Your thoughts have become meditation if whatever thought or perception occurs, without having to be abandoned, turns into the meditation training simply by embracing it with mindfulness. They have not become meditation if you need to meditate by withholding them.

The qualities have arisen in you if you attain the signs such as turning away from the eight worldly concerns. They have not arisen if your mind isn't pliable.

You have planted the seed of the form-bodies if during the ensuing certainty you feel compassion for sentient beings and make aspirations to benefit others. You have not planted them if it feels difficult to be compassionate.

You will have attained mastery over the relative state if during the ensuing certainty, you feel sure of the unfailing details of causation. You have not attained it if you fail to gain certainty in the dependency of causation.

❧

At the time of lesser One-Pointedness, you have a definite meditative state of mind that is an aware emptiness endowed with bliss experience. When a thought or perception occurs within that experience, it dissolves and is liberated by itself. You may perhaps have the intellectually fabricated certainty of thinking, "This is the meditation!"

རྨི་ལམ་གསལ་དྭངས་ཐོན་ཙམ་ལས་ཁྱད་ཆེར་མི་འོང་། འགའ་ཞིག་ལ་རྨི་གྲངས་མང་ལ་ངེས་བཟུང་རྒྱུང་བའོ།།

རེས་མཉམ་པར་འཇོག་དཀའ་ཞིང་སྒོམ་མི་འོང་བ་འདྲ་སྙམ་པའང་འབྱུང་། འཕེལ་འགྲིབ་ཆེ་མོས་གུས་དག་སྣང་སྙིང་རྗེ་རྣམས་སྐྱོའོ།།

རྩེ་གཅིག་འབྲིང་གི་དུས་གསལ་སྟོང་བདེ་ཉམས་དང་བཅས་པའི་སྒོམ་དེ་ནམ་སྒོམ་སྒོམ་བརྟན་པོ་འབྱུང་ཞིང་རེས་མ་བསྒོམས་ཀྱང་དེའི་ངང་དུ་ཆམ་གྱིས་འགྲོ། ཉམས་དེའི་ངང་ནས་རྟོག་སྣང་འཆར་བ་སྤར་བས་ཞུང་ཞིང་གང་ཤར་རང་དྭངས་སུ་འགྲོ།

རྗེས་སྣང་དུ་གསལ་སྟོང་གི་ཉམས་དང་བཅས་པའི་སྣང་བ་གྱུ་ཡངས་སང་ངེ་བ་འབྱུང་། རེས་ཨ་འཐས་སུའང་འཆར།

རྗེས་ཤེས་སུ་ནམ་དྲན་སྒོམ་དུ་ཆམ་གྱིས་འགྲོ། རྨི་ལམ་དུ་ཉམས་དེས་རེས་སླིབ་རེས་མི་སླིབ་འགའ་ཞིག་ལ་རྨི་གྲངས་ཉུང་དུ་འགྲོ་བ་འོང་། སྒོམ་ལ་སྤྲོ་བ་སྐྱོའོ།།

རྩེ་གཅིག་ཆེན་པོའི་དུས་གསལ་སྟོང་བདེ་ཉམས་དང་བཅས་པ་རྒྱུན་ཆད་མེད་པར་འཆར་ཞིང་།

རྣམ་རྟོག་ཐམས་ཅད་དེའི་ངང་དུ་ཐིམ་རྗེས་སྣང་ཐམས་ཅད་དེའི་ངང་དུ་སོང་རྨི་ལམ་ཕལ་ཆེར་ཡང་དེའི་ངང་རྒྱུད་དེ།

During the ensuing perceptions, you perceive them with a sense of delight, but for the most part they are a solid reality.

During the ensuing certainty, whenever you embrace it with a mindful presence, you have an experience of aware emptiness, but it is accompanied by the attitude of thinking, "This is empty! This is a mental experience!"

During the dream state, apart from a slightly higher degree of lucidity, there isn't much difference. Some people have a greater number of dreams, but not very specific.

Sometimes you find it hard to remain in composure and think, "My meditation is not succeeding!" There are considerable fluctuations, and you feel devotion, pure perception and compassion.

At the time of medium One-Pointedness, your training in aware emptiness accompanied by a feeling of bliss grows stable whenever you practice. Sometimes you arrive in it suddenly, even without practicing.

Within that state of experience, fewer thoughts and perceptions arise than before, and they are liberated by themselves.

During the ensuing perceptions, they are accompanied by the experience of aware emptiness, and they feel open and free. Sometimes they are also felt as solid reality.

During the ensuing certainty, you arrive totally in the meditation training whenever you remember.

During the dream state, sometimes the meditation-moods happen, sometimes not. For some people dreams grow less in number.

བཟང་ཞེན་གྱི་འཛིན་པ་དང་བཅས་པའི་ངེས་ཤེས་ལ་སེམས་བདེ་སྟོང་རིག་སྟོང་རྣམ་རྟོག་གསལ་སྟོང་སྣང་བ་སྣང་སྟོང་སོགས་ཀྱི་སྟོང་ཉམས་དང་ཐམས་ཅད་རྨི་ལམ་སྒྱུ་མ་ལྟ་བུ་སོགས་ཀྱི་མྱོང་བ་མང་པོ་འཆར།

ཟག་བཅས་ཀྱི་ཡོན་ཏན་འགའ་རེའང་སྐྱེ།

སྒོམ་འདི་བས་བཟང་བ་མེད་སྙམ་པ་འོང་ཞིང་མོས་གུས་སོགས་སྐྱེའོ།།

དེ་ཡང་རྩེ་གཅིག་གསུམ་གྱི་དུས་སུ་རི་མཚམས་དང་འདག་སྦྱར་དང་སྨྲ་བཅད་ལ་བརྩོན་པར་བྱ་གྲིབ་ལ་འཛེམ་ཞིང་གྲིབ་ཕོག་ན་གྲིབ་སེལ་བྱ།

བྱིང་རྒོད་བྱུང་ན་སྐྱོན་བསལ་བ་དང་ངོ་ལྟ་བྱ།

རྨུགས་ན་སྡིག་བཤགས་བྱ་ཞིང་བླ་མ་ལ་དབང་ཞུ།

ཏིང་ངེ་འཛིན་གྱི་དབང་མང་དུ་བླང་། ཚོགས་འཁོར་དང་མཆོད་འབུལ་དང་སྦྱིན་གཏོང་བྱ་ཞིང་བླ་མ་དང་མཆེད་གྲོགས་ལ་ཞུས་ཏེ་བཅོས།

ཏ་ཅང་སྐྱོན་ཆེ་ཞིང་བླ་མ་དང་མཆེད་གྲོགས་ལ་ཞུ་མི་འདོད་པ་དང་ལོག་ལྟ་སྐྱེས་པ་བྱུང་ན་བདུད་ཀྱི་བར་ཆད་ཡིན་པས་སྐྱབས་འགྲོ་བྱ།

You begin to take delight in your meditation training.

At the time of greater One-Pointedness, the aware emptiness accompanied by the bliss experience becomes constant, and all your thoughts dissolve into that state. All ensuing perceptions take place within that. Dreams, for the most part, are also included within that state.

You gain an assurance that retains a fondness for eminence. You may also have various meditative moods of emptiness: that mind is a blissful emptiness, an empty knowing, that thoughts are an aware emptiness and that appearances are a perceived emptiness. Or you may have the experience that everything is like a dream and magical illusion. You may also manifest some conditioned virtues. You may begin to think, "There is no meditation state superior to this!" You also feel devotion and so forth.

During these three stages of One-Pointedness, exert yourself in staying in mountain retreats, sealing off your room and keeping silence. Beware of becoming defiled, and perform the rituals for cleansing defilement if you do come into contact with such defilements.

When you feel dull or agitated, remove these faults and look into mind essence. When you feel obscured, apologize for misdeeds and request empowerment from your master. Receive the samadhi-empowerments repeatedly. Offer feasts, make offerings and give alms. Ask advice from your master and Dharma friends, and correct your practice.

སྒྲོ་ཤས་ངེས་འབྱུང་མོས་གུས་དག་སྣང་སྙིང་རྗེ་རྣམས་རྒྱལ་ཕྱུང་སྟེ་བསྒོམ། ཞག་འགའ་ཟུང་དུབ་བསང་བྱས་ལ་སྐྱོན་བཅོས་ཤིང་བསྐྱང་བ་དང་ལུས་སྦྱོང་ཅི་རིགས་བྱའོ།།

དེ་ལྟར་ཏིང་ངེ་འཛིན་དེ་སྔར་བཤད་པའི་སྐྱོང་ཐབས་ལྟར་འཇུར་དྲན་ནམ་བཟུང་དྲན་གྱིས་རྩེ་གཅིག་ཏུ་སྐྱོང་།

རྟོག་དཔྱོད་ཀྱི་གོ་ཡུལ་དང་མི་རྟོག་པའི་གནས་པ་དང་མྱོང་བའི་ཉམས་དང་རྗེས་ཤེས་ཀྱི་སྣང་ཤས་རྣམས་སུ་མ་ཤོར་བར་བྱ།

ཉམས་བཟང་བ་ལ་དགའ་ཆོར་གྱི་ཞེན་འཛིན་དང་ངན་པ་ལ་མི་དགའ་བའི་སྐྱོན་བལྟས་མི་བྱ། གང་ཤར་ཡང་སྤང་བླང་མེད་པར་འཛིན་མེད་བཅོས་མེད་དུ་སྐྱོང་། ཉམས་འཕྲུག་ན་ཉམས་དང་བྲལ་ཏེ་ངར་བསྐྱེད་ལ་ཤེས་པ་སོ་མ་ཡང་ཡང་སྐྱོང་། སྐབས་སུ་སྒྲུབ་བརྒྱུད་གོང་མས་སྒྲུབ་ཚུགས་བཟུང་བའི་རྣམ་ཐར་དང་རྗེ་རྗེའི་མགུར་ལ་སོགས་པ་ཡང་བལྟས་ཏེ་རང་ཡང་དེ་ལྟ་བུའི་སྙིང་སྟོབས་བསྐྱེད་པ་སོགས་བྱའོ།།

དེ་ལྟར་བསྐྱངས་པས་བདེ་གསལ་མི་རྟོག་པ་གསུམ་དབྱེར་མེད་པ་སེམས་ཀྱི་རང་བཞིན་གསལ་སྟོང་དུ་འདུག་པ་མྱོང་ཞིང་རྟོགས་ཏེ།

རྣམ་རྟོག་གསལ་སྟོང་དང་སྣང་བ་སྣང་སྟོང་དུ་རྟོགས་ཤིང་ཐམས་ཅད་སེམས་སུ་ཐག་ཆོད་པ་དང་། སེམས་སྐྱེ་མེད་རང་རིག་དང་རང་གྲོལ་དུ་རྟོགས་ཏེ་རྩེ་གཅིག་གི་རྟོགས་པ་མཐར་ཕྱིན་པར་འགྱུར་རོ།།

If it happens that your shortcoming is so severe that you do not want to ask advice from your master or Dharma friends and you begin to foster wrong views, since this is an obstacle from Mara, you should take refuge.

Continue your practice while bringing forth an even deeper weariness and renunciation, devotion, pure perception and compassion. For a few days take a rest, correct the shortcomings and then continue. Do any appropriate physical exercises. In this way, carry on one-pointedly according to the way of sustaining samadhi explained above, with vigorous mindfulness or a tenacious mindful presence.

Take care not to stray into intellectual analysis, thoughtless calm, savoring a meditative experience or hankering after the ensuing certainty.

Do not cling fondly to nice experiences, while regarding unpleasant experiences as undesirable defects. Do not accept or reject, no matter what occurs, but train in being free from fixating and the attempt to correct.

If the meditative mood is dense, disconnect yourself from it by sharpening your attention, and repeatedly train in fresh wakefulness.

At times, read the life-stories about how the forefathers of the Practice Lineage maintained their meditation practice, their vajra songs and so forth, and by doing so develop the fortitude to emulate them.

Continuing your practice in this way, you experience and then realize that bliss, clarity and nonthought are indivisible as the empty and aware nature of mind. You re-

ཅེས་ཀྱང་བོགས་མ་བྱུང་ན་ཞེན་པ་གསུམ་བཏང་བར་བྱ་སྟེ།

བདག་ཏུ་ཞེན་པ་བཏང་བ་ནི། ཚེ་འདིའི་ལྟོས་ཐག་བཅད་མི་ཁྲུ་ནས་ཕུད་འཛིག་རྟེན་གྱི་འཁྲི་བ་བཏང་། དགྲ་གཉེན་གྱི་ཆགས་སྡང་དང་ལུས་བླ་མ་ལ་དབུལ་ཕུང་པོའི་གཅེས་འཛིན་སྤང་ཀུ་སུ་ལུའི་མཆོད་སྦྱིན་བྱ།

ཡོངས་སྤྱོད་ལ་ཞེན་པ་བཏང་བ་ནི། ནོར་རྫས་ཅི་ཡོད་པ་བླ་མ་མཉེས་པའི་འབུལ་བ། ཡི་དམ་ལ་སོགས་མཉེས་པའི་མཆོད་གཏོར་དང་ཚོགས་འཁོར། ཇོ་རྗེས་སྦྱིན་མཉེས་པའི་སྦྱོང་དག་བྱས་ལ།

སྐྱིད་འདོད་ཟ་འདོད་འགྱུར་འདོད་ཀྱི་འཛོམ་ཤ་བློས་བཏང་། ལྟོ་གོས་གཏམ་གསུམ་ཁྲིད་ཏུ་བསད།

སྔར་བཤད་པའི་རི་དྭགས་ལྟ་བུའི་སྤྱོད་པ་ལ་སོགས་བྱ་ཞིང་ཆགས་སྡང་དང་གཡེང་བ་ཅན་གྱི་གནས་ཕ་ཡུལ་སོགས་སྤང་། ཅེས་ཀྱང་སྤང་མ་ཚུགས་ན་ལོ་ཤས་སྨྲ་བཅད་བྱ།

ཏིང་ངེ་འཛིན་ལ་ཞེན་པ་བཏང་བ་ནི། དགའ་ཞིང་སྤྲོ་ལ་ཡིད་ཆེས་པའི་བཟང་ཉམས་ཐམས་ཅད་གཏོང་། གནས་ལུགས་གང་ཤར་ལ་བཟང་ངན་མེད་པར་ཐག་བཅད་དེ་ལ་བཞག།

ཤེས་པ་ཉམས་དང་བྲལ་བའི་རྗེན་པ་རྣལ་མ་བསྐྱང་བས་རིམ་གྱིས་བོགས་ཐོན་ཏེ་ཅི་ཞིག་ན་ཉམས་སྐྱོང་དེ་དག་ནས་ཡུལ་དང་ཡུལ་ཅན་གྱི་གཉིས་འཛིན་ཞིག་སྟེ།

alize that thoughts are aware emptiness, that perceptions are perceived emptiness, and thus you resolve that everything is mind. Realizing this mind to be a nonarising self-knowing that is self-liberated, you have completed the realization of One-Pointedness.

If for some reason you do not progress at all, you should train in giving up the three types of clinging:

Giving up the clinging to I. Cast away all concerns for this life. Be an outcast from human society. Sever worldly ties. Throw away attachment to friends and hostility to enemies. Offer your body to your guru. Abandon the cherishing of the physical aggregates. Make the *kusulu* offering.

Giving up the clinging to possessions. Make a pleasing offering to your master of all your wealth and belongings. Make pleasing torma and feast offerings to your yidam and so forth. Give pleasing presents to your vajra brothers and sisters. Give up hoping for happy times, good meals and nice things. Forgo food, clothing and good reputation. Keep to the above-mentioned conduct of a mountain deer and so forth, and forsake your homeland and other places that promote distraction, attachment and aggression. If for some reason you cannot forsake those places, then keep silent for a couple of years.

Giving up the clinging to samadhi. Discard taking delight in, enjoying or trusting all "good" experiences. Transcend into the natural state by resolving that whatever occurs is

སེམས་ཀྱི་ངོ་བོ་སྐྱེ་འགག་གི་སྤྲོས་པ་དང་བྲལ་བར་རྟོགས་ཏེ་སྤྲོས་བྲལ་གྱི་རྟོགས་པ་འཆར་རོ།།

གསུམ་པ་ནི། སྤྲོས་བྲལ་ལ་ཡང་གསུམ་སྟེ།

རྟོག་སྣང་སེམས་ཀྱི་ངོ་བོ་སྐྱེ་འགག་གི་སྤྲོས་པ་དང་བྲལ་བར་རྟོགས་ཀྱང་སྟོང་པར་འཛིན་པའི་ངེས་ཤེས་ཀྱི་སྦྱོང་འཕྲིས་དང་མ་བྲལ་ཞིང་འཁོར་འདས་ལ་རེ་དོགས་ཡོད་པ་སྤྲོས་བྲལ་ཆུང་ངུ།

སྟོང་འཛིན་ངེས་ཤེས་ཀྱི་སྦྱོང་འཕྲིས་དག་ཀྱང་སྣང་ཐོག་ཏུ་རེ་དོགས་འོང་ཞིང་སྒྲོ་འདོགས་མ་ཆོད་པ་སྤྲོས་བྲལ་འབྲིང་པོ།

སྣང་སྲིད་འཁོར་འདས་ཐམས་ཅད་ལ་སྟོང་འཛིན་ངེས་ཤེས་ཀྱི་འཛིན་པ་གྲོལ་ནས་རེ་དོགས་དང་བྲལ་ཞིང་སྒྲོ་འདོགས་ཆོད་པ་སྤྲོས་བྲལ་ཆེན་པོའོ།།

སྤྲོས་བྲལ་མཐར་ཕྱིན་མ་ཕྱིན་གྱི་དབྱེ་བ་ནི། དེ་ལ་སེམས་ཀྱི་ངོ་བོ་སྤྲོས་བྲལ་ཏུ་མཐོང་བ་ལ་ངེས་ཤེས་ཀྱི་འཛིན་པ་གྲོལ།

སྦྱོང་ཚོར་མཁན་པོའི་རྒྱ་བ་ཆོད་ནས་སྤྲོས་པ་ཐམས་ཅད་དག་པའི་ངང་དུ་ཕྱལ་གྱིས་སོང་ན་སྤྲོས་བྲལ་གྱི་ངོ་བོ་མཐོང་།

neither good nor bad. Maintain a wakefulness that is natural and naked, stripped of any meditative mood.

By doing so, you gradually progress and, at some point, your meditation-moods dissolve. The dualistic fixating on subject and object falls apart. You realize that the essence of mind is free from the constructs of arising and ceasing. Thus, the realization of Simplicity dawns.[18]

Simplicity and Its Enhancement

Simplicity also has three stages. The lesser Simplicity is when you realize that the identity of the thinking and perceiving mind is devoid of such constructs as arising and ceasing. However, you are not free from the fetter of savoring the conviction that clings to it as being empty. You also still entertain hopes and fears concerning samsara and nirvana.

The medium Simplicity is when the fetter of savoring this conviction that clings to it as being empty has dissolved. But, you have hopes and fears during perceptions and have not cleared up uncertainties.

The greater Simplicity is when you have dissolved the fixating on the conviction that all of samsara and nirvana — whatever appears and exists — is empty. You are free from hope and fear, and you have cleared up uncertainties.

These are the distinctions as to whether or not the perfection of Simplicity has been reached:

སྟོང་འཛིན་ཉམས་ཀྱི་དྲི་མ་ངེས་ཤེས་ཀྱི་ཆ་མ་དག་ན་ངོ་བོ་མ་མཐོང་།

རེ་དོགས་དང་སྟོང་འཛིན་གྱི་ཆ་ཙམ་ཡང་མེད་པར་ཐ་མལ་ཤེས་པ་སྤྲོས་བྲལ་དུ་སྒྲོ་འདོགས་ཆོད་ན་རྩལ་རྫོགས།

རང་བཞིན་སྐྱེ་མེད་དུ་ཤེས་ཀྱང་སྣང་ཐོག་ཏུ་རེ་དོགས་འོང་ཞིང་སྟོང་འཛིན་གྱི་འཁྲིས་མ་སངས་ན་རྩལ་མ་རྫོགས།

རྟོག་སྣང་ཐམས་ཅད་སྟོང་འགྱུ་སྟོང་སྣང་དུ་རང་ངོ་ཤེས་ནས་རྗེས་སྣང་དུ་མཉམ་གཞག་གི་རྟོགས་པ་ལྟ་བུར་འཆར་ན་རྣམ་རྟོག་སྒོམ་དུ་ཤར།

དེ་མི་འཆར་ན་མ་ཤར།

ཐབས་ལམ་ལ་གནད་དུ་བསྟུན་ཏེ་གྲུབ་པའི་རྟགས་དང་རྟོགས་པ་འབྲེལ་ན་ཡོན་ཏན་སྐྱེས།

གྲུབ་རྟགས་ཀྱི་སྣང་ཆ་མ་ཐོན་ན་མ་སྐྱེས།

སྟོང་ཉིད་ཀྱི་མ་འགགས་པའི་རྩལ་ལ་དམིགས་མེད་ཀྱི་སྙིང་རྗེས་སྐྱེས་ནས་སེམས་བསྐྱེད་དང་སྨོན་ལམ་གྱི་རྟེན་འབྲེལ་རྗེས་ཤེས་སུ་སྒྲིག་ན་གཟུགས་སྐུའི་ས་བོན་ཐེབས།

སྙིང་རྗེ་སྐྱེ་དཀའ་ཞིང་ཐབས་རྟེན་འབྲེལ་མི་སྒྲིག་ན་ས་བོན་མ་ཐེབས།

In order to see the essence of mind as being free from constructs — simplicity — your clinging to conviction must dissolve. You have seen the essence of Simplicity if you, after investigating thoroughly the nature of the experiencer, totally arrive in a state in which all constructs have dissolved. You have not seen the essence if you have not dissolved the *tarnish of conviction*, which is the experience of clinging to emptiness.

You have perfected the strength of Simplicity if you have cleared up uncertainties about ordinary mind as being devoid of constructs without even the slightest shred of clinging to emptiness, hope or fear. You have not perfected its strength if you entertain hope and fear during perceptions, even though you know their nature to be nonarising and you have not dissolved the clinging to emptiness.

Your thoughts have become meditation if for all thoughts and perceptions you recognize that they are instances of empty thinking and empty perceiving. During the ensuing perceptions, you have a realization that is like that of the meditation state. Your thoughts have not become meditation if that does not happen.

The qualities have arisen if by applying the key points of the *path of means* you connect the signs of accomplishment with realization. The qualities have not arisen if you do not manifest visible signs of accomplishment.

You have planted the seed of the form-bodies if nonconceptual compassion arises out of the unobstructed expression of emptiness and if the coincidence of resolve and

སྟོང་ཉིད་རྒྱུ་འབྲས་སུ་ཤར་ནས་ངོ་བོ་སྤྲོས་པ་དང་བྲལ་ཡང་རྐྱེན་གྱིས་ཅིར་ཡང་སྒྱུར་བར་གོ་ན་ཀུན་རྫོབ་ལ་རང་བྱུང་ཚུད། རྒྱུ་འབྲས་ཀྱི་རྟེན་འབྲེལ་མ་གོ་བར་སྟོང་འཛིན་གྱི་ཁྲིད་དུ་གསོད་ན་རང་བྱུང་མ་ཚུད་དོ།།

དེ་ལ་སྤྲོས་བྲལ་ཆུང་ངུའི་དུས་ཆོས་ཐམས་ཅད་ཀྱི་ངོ་བོ་སྐྱེ་འགག་གནས་གསུམ་གྱི་སྤྲོས་པ་དང་བྲལ་བར་རྟོགས་ཀྱང་ཐམས་ཅད་ལ་སྟོང་པར་འཛིན་པའི་འཛིན་པ་ཅུང་ཟད་ཡོད་ལ།

རྗེས་ཤེས་སུ་དྲན་པས་མ་ཟིན་པའི་དུས་དགྲ་གཉེན་ཆགས་སྡང་གི་འཛིན་པ་ཨ་འཐས་འབྱུང་ཞིང་གཉིད་དང་རྨི་ལམ་ཕལ་ཆེར་ཡང་འཁྲུལ་པ་འབྱུང་།

དགེ་སྦྱོར་མཐོ་དམན་ཆེ་ཞིང་བླ་མ་མཆེད་གྲོགས་དང་དགེ་སྦྱོར་ལ་རེས་དད་པ་དང་ངེས་ཤེས་སྐྱེ་རེས་ཐེ་ཚོམ་སྐྱེ་བ་སྲིད་དོ།།

སྤྲོས་བྲལ་འབྲིང་གི་དུས་སྟོང་འཛིན་ཉམས་ཀྱི་དྲི་མ་དེ་དག་ནས་གང་ལ་ཡང་ཞེན་པ་དང་བྲལ།

རྣམ་རྟོག་གི་རྩ་བ་ཆོད་པས་འགྱུ་ཐོག་ཏུ་སྒྲོ་འདོགས་ཆོད་ཀྱང་སྣང་ཐོག་ཏུ་ཨ་འཐས་ཀྱི་རེ་དོགས་དུམ་རེ་འོང་།

རྗེས་ཤེས་དང་རྨི་ལམ་གྱི་ཆེ་འཁྲུལ་མ་འཁྲུལ་སྣ་ཚོགས་འབྱུང་།

དགེ་སྦྱོར་དང་བླ་མ་མཆེད་གྲོགས་ལ་ཡང་དད་པ་དང་ཐེ་ཚོམ་ལ་སོགས་མཐོ་དམན་དུམ་རེ་འབྱུང་།

aspiration is formed during the ensuing certainty. You have not planted the seeds if it feels difficult to be compassionate and if the coincidence of skillful means is not formed.

You have attained mastery over the relative state if emptiness dawns as cause and effect and if you understand that even though the essence is devoid of constructs it can be changed into anything whatsoever through circumstances. You have not attained mastery if without understanding the coincidence of cause and effect you belittle it while fixating on emptiness.

At the time of lesser Simplicity, you realize that the identity of all phenomena is devoid of the constructs of arising, dwelling and ceasing. Nevertheless, you retain a slight fixation on everything being empty. When you fail to embrace the ensuing certainty with mindful presence, you get involved in solid fixation on love and hate toward friend and enemy. As well, your states of deep sleep and dreaming, for the most part, are still deluded.

There are considerable fluctuations in your spiritual practice, and it is possible that sometimes you have trust in your master, Dharma friends and practice, and that sometimes you feel doubt.

At the time of medium Simplicity, the meditative tarnish of fixation on emptiness dissolves and you are totally free from clinging. Having investigated thoughts thoroughly, you may have cleared up uncertainties about thought-movement, but you still entertain some degree of rigidly clinging to hope and fear during perceptions.

རེས་སངས་རྒྱས་ཐོབ་རྒྱུ་མེད་དམྱལ་བར་སྐྱེ་རྒྱུ་མེད་དམ་སྙམ་པའང་འོང་ངོ་། སྤྲོས་ཐལ་ཆེན་པོའི་དུས་འཁོར་འདས་ཀྱི་ཆོས་ཐམས་ཅད་ཀྱི་རྩ་བ་ཆོད་པས་ཐམས་ཅད་ལ་རེ་དོགས་མེད་ཅིང་སྒྲོ་འདོགས་ཆོད་དེ་ཕྱི་ནང་གི་ཆོས་ཐམས་ཅད་ལ་སྟོང་མི་སྟོང་སོགས་ཀྱི་བདེ་མི་བདེ་མེད་པར་ཕྱལ་གྱིས་འགྲོ།

སྣང་བ་ཐམས་ཅད་སྟོང་ཞིང་བདག་མེད་པར་འཆར། རྗེས་ཤེས་སུ་སྣང་བ་ཐམས་ཅད་རྟོག་པར་དག་པའི་ཤེས་པ་དྭངས་སེང་ངེ་བ་འབའ་ཞིག་ཙུང་མི་འོང་ཡང་རིག་སྟོང་སྣང་སྟོང་གི་ཉམས་བཟང་པོ་དང་བཅས་པའི་ཉིན་པར་གྱི་སྒོམ་ལ་རྒྱུན་ཆད་མེད། འོན་ཀྱང་དྲན་པས་རྒྱུན་ཆད་མེད་པར་ཟིན་པ་ཙུང་མི་འོང་བས་བཟུང་དྲན་རེ་ལ་ལྟོས་དགོས་ཤིང་། རྨི་ལམ་དུ་འཁྲུལ་པ་རང་མཚན་པ་དུམ་རེ་འོང་།

རེས་སངས་རྒྱས་ཐོབ་རྒྱུ་མེད་དམྱལ་བར་འགྲོ་རྒྱུ་མེད་གནས་ལུགས་ཀྱི་དོན་རྟོགས་སྙམ་པའང་འོང་།

གཉིད་ཟབ་པའི་ཆོས་རྣམས་ཀྱང་གོ་ཞིང་སེམས་ཉིད་བླ་མར་འཆར་སྣང་བ་དགེ་སྦྱོར་གྱི་གྲོགས་སུ་འགྲོ། གང་ལ་ཡང་ཞེན་པ་ཆུང་ཆོས་བརྒྱད་ལས་བློ་ལྡོག།

འོན་ཀྱང་ད་ནི་བླ་མ་མི་དགོས་སྙམ་པ་དང་ང་རྒྱལ་དང་སྙོམ་སེམས་དང་གཞན་ལ་ཁྱད་དུ་གསོད་པ་སོགས་འབྱུང་དོགས་ཡོད་དོ།།

During the ensuing certainty and dreams, you experience varieties of delusion and nondelusion. Toward your guru, Dharma friends and practice you also go through various types of ups and downs in terms of trust, doubt and so forth. Sometimes you even have the thoughts, "I wonder if there really is a buddhahood to be attained or a hell to be reborn in?"

At the time of greater Simplicity, you have thoroughly investigated all the phenomena of samsara and nirvana, so you entertain neither hopes nor fears about anything. Having cleared up uncertainties, you are totally free from feeling at ease or not at ease concerning outer and inner phenomena being empty or not. All perceptions are experienced as empty and devoid of a self-entity.

During the ensuing certainty all perceptions are not yet an exclusive state of transparent mind in which thoughts have dissolved. Your daytime meditation training is, however, steadfast as it is accompanied by the good meditative states of empty knowing and empty perceiving.

Even so, since mindful presence has not yet become uninterrupted in the literal sense, you occasionally need to depend on a rigorous mindfulness. During dreams, you still have some degree of ordinary delusion.

From time to time you may even think, "I wonder if there really is a buddhahood to attain or a hell realm to end up in! I wonder if this isn't the realization of the natural state!"

You comprehend even the most profound teachings, experience mind essence as being your guru and perceptions

སྤྲོས་བྲལ་གསུམ་གྱི་ཚོ། ཞེན་པ་གསུམ་བཏང་རི་ཁྲོད་ཤིན་ཏུ་དབེན་པ་བརྟེན་ཞིང་སྒྲུབ་བཅུད་དང་འདག་སྦྱར་ལ་ནན་ཏན་བྱ།

གཏོར་མ་དང་བླ་མའི་གསོལ་འདེབས་ཙམ་མ་གཏོགས་མཚན་བཅས་ཀྱི་དགེ་སྦྱོར་རྣམས་རེ་ཞིག་དོར་ནས་དྲན་པ་ལ་རྩིས་སུ་བྱ་ཞིང་ཡེངས་མེད་དུ་བསྒོམ་པ་གལ་ཆེ།

སྐབས་སུ་མཆོད་སྦྱིན་སོགས་འདུས་བྱས་ཀྱི་དགེ་བ་བསགས་པ་དང་།

བླ་མ་ལ་མོས་གུས་མཆེད་གྲོགས་ལ་དག་སྣང་སེམས་ཅན་ལ་སྙིང་རྗེ་བསྒོམ་ཞིང་རྒྱུ་འབྲས་ཀྱི་རྟེན་འབྲེལ་རྣམས་བསམ།

བླ་མ་དང་མཆེད་གྲོགས་རྟོགས་ལྡན་ལ་ཟབ་མོའི་གླེང་མོ་བྱ་བ་དང་གྲུབ་ཐོབ་བརྒྱུད་པའི་རྡོ་རྗེའི་མགུར་བལྟ་བ་དང་དབྱངས་སུ་བླང་བ་སོགས་བྱ།

ཕལ་ཆེར་དུ་དྲན་པ་རྒྱུན་ཆགས་ཀྱིས་མ་ཡེངས་པ་ཉིད་གལ་ཆེ་ཞིང་དམིགས་བཅས་མང་ན་མི་དགའ།

ཡང་བདེ་ཤེས་ཆུང་ཞིང་འགྲོ་འདོད་དང་ཟ་འདོད་དང་སྙིང་མི་དགའ་བ་སོགས་བྱུང་ན་ཐབས་ལམ་འབར་འཇག་དང་མཆོག་གི་གཏུམ་མོ་དང་ལུས་སྦྱོང་སོགས་ཅི་རིགས་བྱའོ།།

become helpers in your spiritual practice. You feel less clinging to anything and turn away from the eight worldly concerns. Nevertheless, you are in danger of falling prey to conceit, arrogance, disparaging others and of thinking, "Now I don't need a teacher anymore!"

৵

During these three stages of Simplicity, forsake the three types of clinging, keep to extremely secluded mountain areas and exert yourself in keeping silence and staying in sealed-up retreat.

Apart from torma offering and supplications to your guru, it is essential that, for some time, you set aside all types of practice with conceptual attributes while focusing on mindful presence and undistracted training.

Sometimes create conditioned virtue by making offerings and giving alms, training in devotion to your guru, pure appreciation of your Dharma friends, compassion for sentient beings and reflecting on the connection between cause and effect. Discuss the profound meaning of realization with your guru and Dharma friends, read the vajra songs of the siddha lineage, sing them as songs and so forth.

For the most part, the important point is to keep undistracted from a continuous mindful presence. Often people do not like too much conceptual focus.

Sometimes it happens that the blissful feeling is diminished and you want to move on, want to eat or feel unhappy and so forth. You should then make use of a

སྤྲོས་བྲལ་ཆེན་པོར་ཡོར་བསྐྱངས་ཀྱང་བོགས་མ་ཐོན་ན་ཞེན་པ་གསུམ་གཏོང་བ་དབང་ཞུ་བ་ཉམས་ཆགས་བཤགས་པ་སོགས་བྱ་ཞིང་རྟོགས་པ་འཕེལ་བར་གསོལ་བ་གདབ།

རང་ཡི་དམ་དུ་བསྒོམས་ལ་དམྱལ་བའི་སྡུག་བསྔལ་བསམ་ཞིང་དེ་སེམས་སུ་ཐག་བཅད་ལ་སྤྲོས་བྲལ་དུ་མཉམ་པར་བཞག།

དེ་བཞིན་དུ་ལྷའི་བདེ་སྐྱིད་དང་འཁོར་བའི་གནས་ཚུལ་དང་མྱང་འདས་ཀྱི་གནས་ཚུལ་རྣམས་བསམ་ཞིང་སྤྲོས་བྲལ་དུ་མཉམ་པར་བཞག།

རེས་རི་བོའི་རྩེར་ཕྱིན་ལ་སྤྲོས་བྲལ་དུ་གློད།

རེས་མང་པོའི་འདུན་སར་སོང་ལ་སྤྲོས་བྲལ་དུ་གློད།

ལྟུང་ཐུན་རེ་བཟུང་ལ་སྣང་བ་ལ་མིག་ཧ་རེ་བལྟ་ཞིང་སྤྲོས་བྲལ་དུ་གློད་དེ་བསྐྱང་བས་བོགས་འབྱུང་བར་བཤད་དོ།།

དེ་ནས་ཅི་ཞིག་ན་འཁོར་འདས་ཀྱི་ཆོས་ཐམས་ཅད་ལ་སྐྱེ་འགག་གི་སྤྲོས་པ་དང་བྲལ་མ་བྲལ་སྟོང་མི་སྟོང་སྤང་བླང་སོགས་ཀྱི་དགག་སྒྲུབ་མེད་པར་གྲ་མ་ཆག་ཟུར་མ་མཉམས་པར་ཕྱག་རྒྱ་ཆེན་པོར་རོ་གཅིག་ཏུ་རྟོགས་པའི་རྣལ་འབྱོར་འཆར་རོ།།

བཞི་པ་ནི། རོ་གཅིག་ཡའང་གསུམ་སྟེ། དྲན་སྣང་ཐམས་ཅད་སེམས་ཉིད་ཕྱག་རྒྱ་ཆེན་པོར་རོ་གཅིག་ཏུ་རྟོགས་ཀྱང་དེར་མྱོང་ཞིང་འཛིན་པའི་ངེས་ཤེས་ཀྱི་འཕྲིས་ཡོད་པ་རོ་གཅིག་ཆུང་ངུ།

suitable practice connected to the path of means, such as the blazing and dripping, the supreme *tummo*, physical exercise or the like.

If you have no progress at the level of greater Simplicity, even after practicing for years, you should forsake the three types of clinging, request empowerment, apologize for samaya breaches and so forth and pray to deepen your realization.

Imagine the suffering of hell while visualizing yourself as your yidam. Resolve that it is mind, and compose yourself in simplicity. Similarly, bring to mind the pleasure of the gods, the states of samsara, and the nature of nirvana, and compose yourself in simplicity.

Sometimes, go to the top of a mountain and relax into the state of simplicity. Sometimes, go to a place where many people gather and relax into simplicity. Retain the winds for a session, look at appearances with wide-open eyes and relax into simplicity. It is said that by continuing in this way you will have progress.

At some point after this, you will experience the pure and uncontaminated yoga of realizing all the phenomena of samsara and nirvana to be of One Taste, the Mahamudra of being free from accepting and rejecting them as with or without the conceptual constructs of arising and ceasing, empty or not empty and so forth.

One Taste and Its Enhancement

One Taste also has three stages. The lesser One Taste is when you have realized that all thoughts and perceptions

དུ་མ་རོ་གཅིག་ཏུ་སྐྱོང་ཞིང་འཛིན་པའི་ངེས་ཤེས་ཀྱི་དྲི་མ་དག་ནས་སྣང་བ་ཕྱིར་མ་ལུས་སེམས་ནང་དུ་མ་ལུས་པར་སྣང་སེམས་དབྱེར་མེད་ལམ་མེ་བ་མངོན་དུ་གྱུར་པ་རོ་གཅིག་འབྲིང་པོ།

དུ་མ་རོ་གཅིག་ཏུ་རྟོགས་རོ་གཅིག་དུ་མར་ཤར་ཏེ་ཐམས་ཅད་མཉམ་ཉིད་གཞུག་མའི་ངང་དུ་ཞི་བ་རོ་གཅིག་ཆེན་པོའོ།།

རོ་གཅིག་མཐར་ཕྱིན་མ་ཕྱིན་གྱི་དབྱེ་བ་ནི།

གང་ཤར་གྱི་སྣང་བ་ལ་སྤང་བླང་དགག་སྒྲུབ་མེད་པར་མཉམ་ཉིད་གཞུག་མ་ཡུལ་མེད་རང་གསལ་དུ་རང་ངོ་ཤེས་ན་རོ་གཅིག་གི་ངོ་བོ་མཐོང་།

མཉམ་ཉིད་དུ་འདྲེས་རྒྱུ་དང་འདྲེས་པའི་སྐྱོང་འཛིན་ངེས་ཤེས་ཀྱི་འཛིན་པ་འདུག་ན་ངོ་བོ་མ་མཐོང་།

གང་ཤར་ཐམས་ཅད་མཉམ་ཉིད་གཞུག་མ་དེའི་རྩལ་དུ་འཆར་ན་རྩལ་རྫོགས། གཉེན་པོའི་འཁྲིས་དང་བཅས་པས་རོ་གཅིག་དུ་མར་མི་འཆར་ན་རྩལ་མ་རྫོགས།

སྣང་སེམས་སོགས་གཉིས་སྣང་གི་འཛིན་པ་དག་སྟེ་ཚོགས་དྲུག་གི་འཆར་སྒོ་ལ་འཆིང་གྲོལ་མེད་པར་གང་ཤར་གྱིས་ཚོག་ན་རྣམ་རྟོག་སྒོམ་དུ་ཤར།

are of one taste in being the Mahamudra of mind essence. However, you still retain a bind: the conviction of savoring and clinging to that.

The medium One Taste is when this tarnish has dissolved: the conviction of savoring and clinging to multiplicity as being one taste. You have actualized the resplendent indivisibility of perceptions and mind in which the perceived is not held as being outside and mind is not held as being inside.

The greater One Taste is when you realize multiplicity as being of one taste and you experience one taste as being multiplicity. Thus, everything subsides into the original state of equality.

ঌ

Here are the distinctions as to whether or not perfection in One Taste has been reached:

You have seen the essence of One Taste if, free from accepting or rejecting, confirming or denying anything perceived, you have recognized the original state of equality as an objectless natural awareness. You have not seen the essence if you still cling to the conviction that savors this equality in terms of something to be mingled and a mingling with it.

You have perfected the strength of One Taste if whatever you encounter is experienced as the expression of this original state of equality. You have not perfected its strength if one taste isn't experienced as multiplicity because of retaining the bind of a remedy.

འཆར་སྒོ་རྣམས་ངོ་ཤེས་ཀྱི་དྲན་པས་གྲོལ་དགོས་ན་མ་ཤར།

སྣང་སེམས་འདྲེས་ནས་སྤྲུལ་བསྒྱུར་ལ་སོགས་པའི་རྫུ་འཕྲུལ་ཐོབ་ན་ཡོན་ཏན་སྐྱེས། སད་བྱེད་ལམ་གྱི་རྐྱེན་ཞན་ནས་རྟགས་མ་ཐོན་ན་ཡོན་ཏན་མ་སྐྱེས།

ཀུན་ཁྱབ་ཀྱི་སྙིང་རྗེ་རྩོལ་མེད་དུ་འབྱུང་ཞིང་གཞན་དོན་གྱི་གཏེར་ཁ་བྱེ་ན་གཟུགས་སྐུའི་ས་བོན་ཐེབས། སྙིང་རྗེ་སོགས་ཐབས་ཀྱི་ནུས་པ་ཆུང་ཞིང་གཞན་དོན་མི་འགྲུབ་ན་ས་བོན་མ་ཐེབས།

རྒྱུ་འབྲས་ཀྱི་རྟེན་འབྲེལ་གསལ་བར་རྟོགས་པས་རིག་པ་སྐད་ཅིག་མའི་འཆར་སྒོས་འཁོར་འདས་ཀྱི་གྲེས་སོ་བྱེད་པར་ཤེས་ཏེ་རྒྱུ་འབྲས་ལ་མཁས་ན་ཀུན་རྫོབ་རང་བྱན་ཚུད། ངོ་གཅིག་ཏུ་མའི་རྒྱུ་འབྲས་སུ་མ་འཆར་ན་རང་བྱན་མ་ཚུད་པའོ།།

དེ་ལ་རོ་གཅིག་ཆུང་ངུའི་དུས་ཐམས་ཅད་གཉུག་མའི་ངོ་བོར་རྟོགས་ཀྱང་དེར་སྤྱོད་རྒྱུ་དང་དེར་འཛིན་པའི་ཆ་ཙུང་ཟད་ཡོད་ལ།

རྗེས་ཤེས་སུ་ཡུལ་རྐྱེན་དྲག་པོས་དཀྲུགས་པའི་ཚོགས་དྲུག་གི་སྣང་བ་ལ་དགེ་སྦྱོར་དུ་མི་བདེ་བ་འོང་ཞིང་རང་ཁར་ཡང་གཟུང་འཛིན་ཨ་འཐས་ཀྱི་སྣང་བ་དུམ་རེ་འབྱུང་།

Your thoughts have become meditation if all dualistic clinging, including mind and the perceived, etc. has dissolved. Hence — free from the sense of being bound or released in the six types of impressions — it is all right to let whatever appears appear. They have not become meditation if you need to liberate the impressions with a reminder to recognize.

The qualities have arisen if, after mingling mind and perceptions, you have attained miraculous powers, such as being able to conjure and multiply. The qualities have not arisen if the signs fail to appear due to the inducing circumstances of the path being feeble.[19]

You have planted the seed of the form-bodies if all-embracing compassion occurs effortlessly and the treasure-mine of benefiting others has opened. You have not planted this if the power of means, such as compassion, is weak and if you do not accomplish the benefit of others.

You will have attained mastery over the relative state if you have become skilled in causation. This means you can separate samsara and nirvana by experiencing the immediacy of awareness because of clearly realizing the dependent connection between causes and effects. You have not attained this mastery if you do not experience one taste as being the causation of multiplicity.

❧

At all times during the lesser One Taste, you have realized the essence of the original state, but you still retain

རྨི་ལམ་ན་ཡང་འཁྲུལ་པ་དང་འཛིན་པ་དུམ་རེ་འོང་།

དེས་ལུས་སྣང་སེམས་གསུམ་དབྱེར་མེད་པའི་ཉམས་སྐྱེ།

འོན་ཀྱང་རྒྱུ་འབྲས་ལ་རྩེ་འཛོག་དང་མོས་གུས་དང་སྙིང་རྗེ་ཆུང་དུ་འགྲོ་བ་སྲིད་དོ།།

རོ་གཅིག་འབྲིང་གི་དུས་རྟོགས་བྱ་རྟོགས་བྱེད་སྤྱོད་བྱ་སྤྱོད་བྱེད་ཀྱི་འཛིན་པ་གྲོལ་སྣང་སེམས་གཉིས་འཛིན་གྱི་རྩ་བ་ཆོད།

རྗེས་ཤེས་དང་རྨི་ལམ་ཡང་སྔར་བས་འཁྲུལ་པ་ཆུང་ཞིང་ཨ་འཐས་ཀྱི་འཛིན་པ་ཡང་ཆེར་མི་འོང་།

རོ་གཅིག་ཆེན་པོའི་དུས་མཉམ་ཉིད་གཞུག་མ་མ་འགགས་པའི་རྩལ་སྣ་ཚོགས་ལ་བདེན་འཛིན་དང་བྲལ་བའི་གཉིས་མེད་ཀྱི་རྟོགས་པ་དེ་ཉིད་ཉིན་མཚན་འཁོར་མོར་འབྱུང་།

མི་རྟོག་པའི་འཆར་སྒོ་སྣང་ལ་མ་ངེས་པའི་གསལ་ཙམ་གྱི་སྤྱོད་ཚོར་ཙུང་ཟད་རེ་འབྱུང་།

རྗེས་ཤེས་སུ་སྣང་བ་འཛིན་མེད་གསལ་སྟོང་སྒྱུ་མ་ལྟ་བུར་སྣང་ཞིང་ཤེས་བཞིན་གཉིས་སྣང་ཕྲ་མོ་འཆར། འཛིན་མེད་ཀྱི་རྨི་ལམ་འལ་འོལ་འགག་མེད་དུ་འབྱུང་། དེས་རྨི་ལམ་མེད་པ་ཡང་འོང་བར་བཤད་དོ།།

a slight sense that it is something to be savored and held on to.

During the ensuing certainty, you find difficulty in continuing your spiritual practices while encountering perceptions disturbed by intense objects and circumstances, and you, to a minor degree, experience a solid fixation on duality.

During the dream state, there is some slight confusion and clinging.

Sometimes you have the experience that all three — your body, perceptions and mind — are indivisible. However, it is possible that your regard for causation, your devotion and your compassion may dwindle.

At the time of medium One Taste, the clinging to the subject and object of realization, the experiencer and the experienced, dissolve. The fixation on the duality of mind and perceptions is cut at its root.

During the ensuing certainty and the dream state your confusion is even less than before, and you have no noticeable clinging to solid reality.

At the time of greater One Taste, your realization of nonduality becomes constant throughout day and night, and it is free from clinging to the manifold unobstructed expressions of the original state of equality as being real.

The experience of nonthought, as simply an aware quality that perceives yet does not judge, occurs with a slight savoring.

During the ensuing certainty, you perceive with a subtle duality and appreciate appearances as being like a magical

རོ་གཅིག་གསུམ་གྱི་ཚེ་གནས་ཕལ་ཆེར་དབེན་པ་བསྟེན། རེས་འགའ་ཙམ་ཚོགས་སུ་ཡང་བསྡད་ལ་བོགས་དབྱུང་།

བསྒོམ་མ་བསྒོམ་ཁྱད་མེད་སྐམ་ཡང་དབེན་པ་བསྟེན་ཞིང་ཡང་དག་གི་དྲན་པ་སྒོམ་པ་ཉིད་དུ་གནད་ཆེའོ།།

རོ་གཅིག་ཆེན་པོའི་རྟོགས་པ་ཐོབ་ཀྱང་། མངོན་ཤེས་ཕྲ་མོ་དང་མཁའ་འགྲོའི་མཚན་མ་མ་བྱུང་ན་ཉམས་གྲིབ་ཕོག་པ་ཡིན་པས་ཚ་ཚ་སྟོང་རྩ་སོགས་བཏབ་ཅིང་དེ་རེ་རེ་ལ་མེ་ཏོག་རེ་ཕུལ་ལ།

བདག་གི་གྲིབ་ཉེ་བར་ཞི་བར་མཛད་དུ་གསོལ་ཞེས་གསོལ་བ་བཏབ།

གཞན་ཡང་གྲིབ་སེལ་གྱི་གཟུངས་ཆོག་དང་དགེ་བའི་སྣ་ཅི་རིགས་བྱ།

མཚན་མ་བྱུང་ནས་དགའ་མི་དགའ་འདུག་ན་བདུད་ཞུགས་པ་ཡིན་པས་ཕན་འདོགས་པ་དང་གནོད་པ་སྐྱེལ་བ་དང་བདུད་ལ་སོགས་པ་ཐམས་ཅད་རང་གི་སེམས་ཡིན་སེམས་ནམ་མཁའ་ལྟར་མཐའ་དབུས་མེད་སྐམ་དུ་བསམ།

ལར་རོ་གཅིག་སྐྱེས་ནས་རྟོགས་པ་ལ་མི་འཇིགས་ཡོན་ཏན་ལ་མི་དགའ་སྐྱོན་གྱིས་ཁ་བྲིད་ཀྱང་མི་ནུས་པ་ཡིན།

སླར་ལ་ཕྲག་དོག་ཆེ་ཉོན་མོངས་མང་རྣམ་རྟོག་རགས་ཟུར་མགོ་རྟེ་དགའ་མི་དགའ་འདུག་ན་བདུད་སེམས་ལ་ཞུགས་པ་ཡིན་པས་དེ་ངོ་ཤེས་པར་བྱས་ལ་དགེ་སྦྱོར་ལ་རིམ་པར་བྱ།

illusion, an aware emptiness in which there is nothing to be held.

Dreams free from clinging occur as unobstructed and ephemeral. It is also taught that at times there are no dreams at all.

During these three stages of One Taste, for the most part, keep to secluded places. From time to time, participate in group gatherings and you will progress.

Even though you think that it makes no difference whether or not you meditate, it is essential to keep to seclusion and train in the true mindful presence.

Even though you have attained the realization of greater One Taste, if you fail to have some degree of clairvoyance and receive signs from the dakinis, you must be tainted by damaged samayas. Therefore, make, for instance, a thousand *tsa-tsas* or the like, and offer a flower to each of them. Make the request, "May my defilement utterly subside!" Perform the *dharani*-ritual for purifying defilement, as well as any other suitable virtuous practice.

If you get involved in pleasure or displeasure when signs occur, you are influenced by Mara. Consider that being benefited or harmed, assisted or hurt by Mara, and so forth, are all your own mind and that this mind is limitless and centerless, like space.

Once the realization of One Taste has dawned within you, there is no fear of thought, no preference toward

ལར་སྒོམ་དང་མི་མཐུན་པ་ཐམས་ཅད་བདུད་རང་དུ་ཤེས་པར་བྱ་ཞེས་གསུངས་པ་ལྟར་གོ་བར་བྱ་ཞིང་།

སེམས་ཅན་ཡང་རང་སེམས་བླ་མ་ཡང་རང་སེམས་སུ་འདུག་པས་སྙིང་རྗེ་དང་མོས་གུས་མི་དགོས་སྐམ་ནས་ཐབས་ཁྱད་དུ་གསོད་སྲིད་པས་སྙིང་རྗེ་དང་མོས་གུས་སོགས་ཀྱི་སྟོབས་བསྐྱེད།

རྟེན་འབྲེལ་བཟང་པོ་ཐམས་ཅད་བསྒྲིག་པ་དང་ངན་པ་ཐམས་ཅད་སྤང་པ་དང་རྒྱུ་འབྲས་ཀྱི་གོ་ཆ་དང་དུ་བླངས་ཏེ་དགེ་སྡིག་གི་བླང་དོར་ཞིབ་ཏུ་བྱ།

གཞན་ལ་ཕན་གནོད་འབྱུང་ཞིང་ལྟའི་ཐུའི་བདུད་ཀྱིས་ཟིན་དོགས་ཡོད་པས་གཞན་དོན་ལྟར་སྣང་སྤང་།

འཁོར་དང་ལོངས་སྤྱོད་དང་སྙན་གྲགས་ལ་མ་ཆགས་པ་གལ་ཆེའོ།།

དེ་ལྟར་བསྒྲུངས་པས་ཉམས་དང་མྱོང་བའི་དྲི་མ་ཐམས་ཅད་དག་ལམ་གྱི་རྟོགས་པ་དང་རང་བཞིན་གྱི་གནས་ལུགས་འདྲེས་ནས་མཉམ་རྗེས་དང་དྲན་པས་ཟིན་མ་ཟིན་མེད་པའི་སྒོམ་མེད་ཀྱི་རྟོགས་པ་འཆར་རོ།།

ལྔ་པ་ནི། སྒོམ་མེད་ལ་ཡང་གསུམ་སྟེ།

དྲན་པས་བཟུང་མ་དགོས་ཆེད་དུ་མཉམ་པར་བཞག་མ་དགོས་པར་སྣང་བ་ཐམས་ཅད་སྒོམ་དུ་འཆར་ཞིང་སྒྱུ་མ་ལྟ་བུའི་འཛིན་པ་ཕྲང་ཟད་ཙམ་སྐྱེ་བ་ཡོད་ཀྱི་བར་སྒོམ་མེད་ཆུང་ངུ།

qualities and you cannot be swayed by faults. On the other hand, Mara has taken possession of your mind if you become profoundly competitive and have plenty of disturbing emotions, obsessive thoughts and preferences. Recognize that and exert yourself in virtuous practices. In any case, understand the meaning of the saying, "Recognize everything that counteracts your meditation training to be Mara."

It is also possible to belittle the importance of methods by thinking, "There is no need for compassion and devotion since sentient beings are my own mind and the guru is also my own mind." Instead, strengthen your compassion and devotion.

Be extremely careful to adopt virtue and avoid evil. Arrange all kinds of positive types of causation, avert all kinds of negative ones, and accept the armor of cause and effect.

When there is benefit or harm happening to others, there is the danger of being caught by the Godly Son Mara, so cast away superficial deeds to benefit others. It is also essential to remain unattached to followers, possessions and fame.

By continuing the practice in this way, the tarnish of meditation-moods and savoring all subside, and the realization of the path and the natural state intermingle. Thus the realization of Nonmeditation dawns beyond composure and postmeditation being embraced or not by mindfulness.

སྒྱུ་མ་ལྟ་བུའི་འཛིན་པ་དེ་དང་ཡང་བྲལ་ཏེ་ཉིན་མཚན་ཐམས་ཅད་སྒོམ་མེད་ཁོར་ཡུག་ཏུ་སོང་ཞིང་རྗེས་སྣང་དུ་རྣམ་ཤེས་ཀྱི་རྒྱུན་ཕྲ་མོ་རང་གསལ་དུ་འཆར་བ་སྒོམ་མེད་འབྲིང་པོ།

རྣམ་ཤེས་ཕྲ་མོ་དེ་ཡང་ཡེ་ཤེས་སུ་གནས་གྱུར་ནས་ཐམས་ཅད་ཡེ་ཤེས་ཀྱི་ཁོར་ཡུག་ཏུ་གྱུར་པ་སྒོམ་མེད་ཆེན་པོའོ།།

སྒོམ་མེད་མཐར་ཕྱིན་མ་ཕྱིན་གྱི་དབྱེ་བ་ནི།

སྒོམ་མེད་ཀྱི་རྟོགས་པ་དེ་ལ་དྲན་རྒྱུའམ་གོམས་རྒྱུ་མེད་པར་སྐྱོང་བ་དག་ན་སྒོམ་མེད་ཀྱི་ངོ་བོ་མཐོང་།

དེ་ལ་དྲན་རྒྱུའམ་གོམས་རྒྱུ་འདུག་ན་ངོ་བོ་མ་མཐོང་།

གཉིས་སྣང་ཕྲ་མོ་དག་ཅིང་ཆོས་ཐམས་ཅད་ཟད་སར་འཁྱོལ་ནས་དུས་ཀུན་ཏུ་ཡེ་ཤེས་དང་དབྱེར་མེད་ན་རྩལ་རྫོགས།

གཉིས་སྣང་ཕྲ་མོ་སྣང་ཞིང་ཤེས་བྱའི་ཆོས་མ་ཟད་ན་རྩལ་མ་རྫོགས།

Nonmeditation and Its Enhancement

Nonmeditation has three stages as well. The lesser Nonmeditation is when all perceptions are experienced as meditation training. You do not have to remain mindful or deliberately compose yourself in the meditation state, and you retain only the slightest clinging to them as being like a magical illusion.

Medium Nonmeditation is when you are even free from this clinging to the notion that they are magical illusions, so that throughout day and night you are in an uninterrupted state of nonmeditation. During the ensuing certainty, a subtle continuity of dualistic consciousness is experienced as natural awareness.[20]

Greater Nonmeditation is when even this subtle dualistic consciousness transforms into original wakefulness, *yeshe*. Everything is simply an overarching state of original wakefulness.

❧

Here are the distinctions as to whether or not perfection in Nonmeditation has been reached:

You have seen the essence of Nonmeditation if your realization of nonmeditation is free from an object of remembering or familiarization so that the savoring has dissolved. You have not seen the essence if you retain a sense of something that needs to be remembered or grown accustomed to.

You have perfected the strength of Nonmeditation if the subtlest dualistic perception has dissolved and you have

ཀུན་གཞིའི་རྣམ་ཤེས་ཐམས་ཅད་མ་སྦྱངས་པར་ཆོས་དབྱིངས་ཡེ་ཤེས་སུ་དག་ན་རྣམ་རྟོག་སྒོམ་དུ་ཤར། རྣམ་རྟོག་གི་འཛིན་པ་བག་ལ་ཉལ་ཕྲ་མོ་དང་ཉམས་མྱོང་གི་དྲི་མ་ཕྲ་མོ་ཞིག་འདུག་ན་ཡང་རྣམ་རྟོག་སྒོམ་དུ་མ་ཤར།

ལུས་འཇའ་ལུས་ཡེ་ཤེས་ཀྱི་གཟུགས་སྐུ་དང་སེམས་འོད་གསལ་ཆོས་སྐུར་ཤར་ནས་ཞིང་ཁམས་དག་པ་རབ་འབྱམས་སུ་སྣང་ན་ཡོན་ཏན་སྐྱེས། ལུས་སེམས་དང་སྣོད་བཅུད་ལ་མ་དག་པའི་སྣང་བ་ཙུང་ཟད་འདུག་ཀྱང་མ་སྐྱེས།

དབྱིངས་དང་ཡེ་ཤེས་དབྱེར་མེད་པའི་ཆོས་ཀྱི་སྐུར་བྱང་ཆུབ་ནས་སྐུ་གསུང་ཐུགས་མི་ཟད་རྒྱན་གྱི་འཁོར་ལོས་སེམས་ཅན་གྱི་དོན་ལྷུན་གྲུབ་ཏུ་རྒྱུན་མི་ཆད་པ་འབྱུང་ན་གཟུགས་སྐུའི་ཕྲིན་ལས་གྲུབ། དེ་ལྟར་མ་གྱུར་པར་ཞིང་ཁམས་དག་པ་ལ་ལྟོས་དགོས་ན་ཕྲིན་ལས་མ་གྲུབ།

སངས་རྒྱས་ཀྱི་ཡོན་ཏན་ཐམས་ཅད་རྫོགས་ན་ཀུན་རྫོབ་དག་ཅིང་བྱང་ཚུད། རྣམ་སྨིན་གྱི་ལུས་རྒྱུ་བག་ཆགས་སྣང་རྒྱུ་རྣམ་ཤེས་སེམས་རྒྱུ་སྟེ་རྒྱུ་གསུམ་གྱིས་སངས་རྒྱས་ཀྱི་ཡོན་ཏན་བསྒྲིབས་ནས་ཀུན་རྫོབ་མ་དག་ཅིང་བྱང་མ་ཚུད་པ་ཡིན་ནོ།།

brought all phenomena to the state of exhaustion, so you are always indivisible from original wakefulness. You have not perfected its strength if you experience even the slightest dualistic perception and you have not exhausted the phenomena of knowable objects.

Your thoughts have become meditation if every instance of all-ground consciousness, without being rejected, has dissolved into being dharmadhatu wisdom. They have not become meditation if you retain a subtle type of propensity for conceptual clinging and the subtle tarnish of savoring an experience.

The qualities have arisen if your body appears as the wisdom *rupakaya* of the rainbow body and your mind as the luminous dharmakaya. Thus the world is experienced as all-encompassing purity. The qualities have not arisen if you retain even the slightest impure perception regarding body and mind, the world and beings.

You have accomplished the activities of the form-bodies if you have reached perfection as the dharmakaya in which basic space and original wakefulness are indivisible, so that your inexhaustible adornment-wheel of Body, Speech and Mind spontaneously and ceaselessly fulfills the needs of sentient beings. You have not accomplished these activities if this has not happened and you still need to depend upon pure realms. You will have purified and attained mastery over the relative state if you have perfected all the qualities of buddhahood. You have not attained this purity and mastery if the three webs obscure the qualities of buddhahood: the body-web of karmic ripening, the per-

དེ་ལ་སྒོམ་མེད་ཆུང་ངུའི་དུས་གཉིས་སྣང་ཞལ་ཆེར་དག་ནས་ཆེད་དུ་སྒོམ་མ་དགོས་དྲན་པས་བཟུང་མ་དགོས་པར་སྣང་བ་ཐམས་ཅད་སྒོམ་དུ་ཤར་ཏེ་སྒོམ་ལས་གཡོ་བ་མེད་པ་འབྱུང་ལ།

རྗེས་སྣང་དུ་མི་རྟོག་ངོ་མ་ཤེས་ཞེས་བྱ་བ་མ་རིག་པའི་ལྷག་མ་ཀུན་གཞིའི་རྣམ་ཤེས་རྟོག་བྲལ་ལུང་མ་བསྟན་དུ་གནས་པ་ཞིག་ཡོང་བ་ལ་གནས་ངན་ལེན་གྱི་དྲི་མ་ཟེར།

ལས་མི་གསོག་ཀྱང་ཡེ་ཤེས་སུ་མ་དག་པའི་འཛིན་པ་སྒྱུ་མ་ལྟ་བུ་ཡང་ཡུད་སྐྱེ་བ་དང་། རྨི་ལམ་དུ་ཡང་ངོ་མ་ཤེས་ཀྱི་བདེན་འཛིན་ཅུང་ཟད་འབྱུང་བར་བཤད་དོ།།

སྒོམ་མེད་འབྲིང་གི་དུས་སྒྱུ་མ་ལྟ་བུའི་གཉིས་སྣང་ཕྲ་མོ་དེ་ཡང་དག་ནས་ཉིན་མཚན་ཐམས་ཅད་སྒོམ་མེད་ཀྱི་འཁོར་ཡུག་ཏུ་འགྱུར་ཞིང་།

རྗེས་སྣང་མི་རྟོག་ངོ་མ་ཤེས་ཀྱི་ཆ་ཕྲ་ཞིང་ཕྲ་བ་རང་གསལ་དུ་ཤར་བ་ཞེས་བྱ་བ་གཤིས་བབས་དང་མཐུན་པར་རྫོགས་པ་ལ་ཟེར་ཏེ་གནས་ངན་ལེན་གྱི་དྲི་མ་ཕྲ་ཞིང་ཕྲ་བ་ཡིན་ལ་མཚན་མོ་ལ་ཡང་དེའི་ཆ་ཡོད་པར་བཤད་དོ།།

སྒོམ་མེད་ཆེན་པོའི་དུས་མི་རྟོག་ངོ་མ་ཤེས་ཀྱི་ཆ་ཕྲ་ཞིང་ཕྲ་བ་དེ་ཡང་ཡེ་ཤེས་སུ་དག་ནས་འོད་གསལ་མ་བུ་འདྲེས་པས་ཐམས་ཅད་ཡེ་ཤེས་ཀྱི་གློང་འབྱམས་སུ་གྱུར་ཏེ་རང་དོན་དུ་ཆོས་སྐུ་རྫོགས་པར་ཐོབ།

ception-web of habitual tendencies and the mind-web of dualistic consciousness.

❧

At the time of lesser Nonmeditation, dualistic perception has mostly dissolved. Without having to deliberately meditate or deliberately remind yourself, all perceptions are experienced as the meditation training, so that you are unwavering from the meditation.

During the ensuing perceptions, there is a remnant of ignorance called *thoughtless nonrecognition*, which is the all-ground consciousness remaining as a thoughtless state of indifference. This is also known as the *defilement of negative tendencies*.

Although you do not create karma, it is taught that clinging, not yet dissolved into original wakefulness, still occurs like fugitive moments of magical illusion. During dreams you still encounter a slight clinging to them as being real due to not recognizing.

At the time of medium Nonmeditation, even this most subtle dualistic perception, which is like a magical illusion, dissolves and you become uninterrupted in the state of nonmeditation throughout day and night.

During the ensuing perceptions, the extremely subtle trait of thoughtless nonrecognition dawns as a natural awareness. This is called *perfection in accordance with the intrinsic nature*. It is taught that this trait is the subtlest defilement of negative tendencies and that it is still present at night.

དེའི་རང་རྒྱལ་ཕྱོགས་མེད་དུ་འབྱོངས་པས་གཞན་དོན་དུ་གཟུགས་སྐུའི་སྣང་བརྙན་གྱིས་འཁོར་བ་ཇི་སྲིད་པར་འགྲོ་བའི་དོན་ལྷུན་གྲུབ་ཏུ་འབྱུང་བར་བཤད་དོ།།

དེ་ལ་ཚེ་འདིར་འཆར་བའི་སྒོམ་མེད་ནི།

སྤྲང་བྱ་སྤྲང་དུ་མེད་གཉེན་པོ་བསྟེན་དུ་མེད་དག་བྱ་རྒྱུ་དང་བྲལ་དག་བྱེད་སེམས་དང་བྲལ་ཤི་མ་ཤི་མེད་པའི་ངེས་པ་གཏིང་ནས་ཐོབ་སྟེ་མཉམ་རྗེས་མེད་པའི་སྒོམ་མེད་ཆུང་འབྲིང་ཅི་རིགས་ལས་འཆར་བར་དཀའ་ལ།

སྤྱིར་སྒོམ་མཁན་བསྒོམ་བྱ་སྒོམ་བྱེད་དང་བྲལ་བའི་སྒོམ་མེད་ཙམ་སྤྲོས་བྲལ་དུ་ཡང་འོང་ཞིང་།

སྣང་བ་དང་རྟོག་པ་སོ་མ་སྒོམ་དུ་ཤར་ནས་མཉམ་རྗེས་མེད་པའི་སྒོམ་མེད་ཙམ་རེ་གཅིག་ཏུ་ཡང་འབྱུང་བས་དེ་དག་ཉམས་ཀྱི་སྒོམ་མེད་ཡིན་གྱི་སྒོམ་མེད་དངོས་མིན་ནོ།།

དེ་ལ་སྒོམ་མེད་དངོས་མི་རྟོག་ངོ་མ་ཤེས་ཀྱི་ཆ་ཕྲ་མོ་རང་གསལ་དུ་མ་ཤར་བར་དུ་དྲན་པ་ཡེ་ཤེས་ཀྱི་འཁོར་ལོས་མ་བཅོས་མི་བསྒོམ་པའི་ཐ་མལ་གྱི་ཤེས་པ་རྒྱུན་བསྲིང་བ་གལ་ཆེ་བར་བཤད་ཅིང་།

At the time of greater Nonmeditation, this extremely subtle trait of thoughtless nonrecognition dissolves into original wakefulness so that the mother and child luminosities intermingle. Everything is now the all-encompassing expanse of original wakefulness so that — for the benefit of yourself — you attain dharmakaya in completeness. Since its natural expression is mastered, free from any partiality, it is taught that the reflections of the form-bodies for the benefit of others will spontaneously fulfill the welfare of beings for as long as samsara lasts.

In this regard, the state of nonmeditation that is experienced during this lifetime is either the lesser or medium Nonmeditation, transcending meditative composure and postmeditation. This is in the sense of attaining the profound certainty that is free from objects to be abandoned and free from a remedy to be applied, free from an object to be purified and free from the mind that purifies, and is beyond dying or not dying. It is difficult to reach higher than that.

Generally speaking, a state of nonmeditation that is the mere absence of meditator, meditation object and the act of meditating also occurs during Simplicity. During One Taste there is also a state of nonmeditation that is merely to experience the freshness of thoughts and perceptions followed by a going beyond meditative composure and postmeditation. These are not the real state of Nonmeditation, but rather the meditation-mood of nonmeditation.

For the real state of Nonmeditation, it is taught that until the subtle trait of *thoughtless nonrecognition* has

གནས་གང་དུ་གནས་གྲོགས་སུ་དང་འགྲོགས་སྤྱོད་པ་ཅི་བྱས་ནའང་ལས་མི་གསོག་ཀྱང་།

སྒོམ་ཆེན་ཆོས་པའི་ཡ་རྒྱལ་བསྐྱང་སྟེ་རི་ཁྲོད་བཟུང་སྒྲུབ་པའི་རྒྱལ་མཚན་བཙུགས་ཅིང་ཚུལ་མིན་གྱི་སྤྱོད་པ་སྤང་བ་དང་ཀུན་རྫོབ་ཀྱི་བླང་དོར་ཚུལ་བཞིན་བྱ་བ་གལ་ཆེའོ།།

མཉམ་བཞག་རྗེས་ཐོབ་རྗེས་ཤེས་སྣང་བ་རྨི་ལམ་གྱི་འཆར་ཚུལ་རྣམས་རིམ་གྱིས་པའི་དབང་དུ་བྱས་པ་ཡིན་ཀྱང་དབེན་པར་སྒོམ་ཉག་གཅིག་སྐྱོང་བ་ལ་བཤད་ཚོད་ལྟར་འབྱུང་མོད་རྗེས་ཐོབ་ཏུ་ཚེ་འདིའི་སྣང་ཤས་ཀྱི་དབང་དུ་བཏང་བ་སོགས་ལ་བཤད་ཚོད་དང་ཁྲིགས་འགྲིགས་པའི་འཆར་ཚུལ་ཐམས་ཅད་ཚུད་མི་འོང་ཡང་རྟོགས་པའི་ངོ་བོ་ཇི་ལྟ་བ་འཆར་རོ།

དེ་ལྟར་རྣལ་འབྱོར་བཅུ་གཉིས་ཀྱི་ཉམས་དང་རྟོགས་པ་འཆར་ཚུལ་ལ་རྣལ་འབྱོར་ཐ་མ་རྣམས་ཤིན་ཏུ་གཏིང་རྟོགས་པར་དཀའ་ཞིང་བློས་དཔྱད་པའི་ཡུལ་མིན་ཀྱང་།

རྗེ་སྒོམ་ཚུལ་གྱི་གསུང་དང་བསྒྲུབ་བརྒྱུད་གོང་མ་འགའི་གསུང་ལ་བརྟེན་པས་ཡིད་ཆེས་པར་བྱའོ།།

dawned as a natural awareness, it is essential to use the mindful presence of continuous wakefulness to sustain the flow of the ordinary mind that is neither contrived nor cultivated.

Even though you do not create any more karma, no matter where you stay, no matter who you are with and no matter what you do, it is essential that as a meditator you maintain the inspiring exterior of a Dharma practitioner. Therefore, keep to mountain retreats, raise the banner of practice, forsake incorrect behavior and deal appropriately with the relative principles of what should be adopted or avoided.

❧

Here I have described the ways in which the meditative composure and the postmeditation, the ensuing certainty, ensuing perceptions and dream states are experienced in terms of the gradual type of person. It is indeed taken as a given that he or she maintains the training one-pointedly in a secluded place. It does not follow all the various ways precisely, such as for instance those who eagerly hanker after mundane appearances during postmeditation. Nevertheless, the identity of the realization may be experienced exactly as it is.

The ways in which the levels of experience and realization of these twelve yogas occur are extremely difficult to fully comprehend for the lesser type of practitioner and are not within the domain of their intellectual scrutiny. Still, you should find trust by means of the teachings of Lord

རྒྱས་པར་བསྒྲུབ་པ་མཐར་བསྐྱལ་ཏེ་ནང་རང་སེམས་ཀྱི་བླ་མ་དང་ཕྱི་གྲུབ་ཐོབ་རྟོགས་ལྡན་གྱི་བླ་མའི་གསུང་དང་མན་ངག་ལས་ཤེས་པར་བྱ་ཞིང་ལར་བློ་ཟད་ཆོས་ཟད་ལ་སྐྱེལ་དགོས་ཀྱི།

རང་ཅག་སྔོན་སྦྱངས་ཀྱི་ལས་འཕྲོ་ཆ་མ་རྫོགས་པར་སྐྱིད་ཆོས་ཀྱིས་སྒོམ་སྒྲུབ་ལོ་འགའ་རེ་བྱས་ནས།

རྟོགས་པ་མངོན་དུ་གྱུར་པར་སློམས་ཏེ་དོན་གཉིས་ལྷུར་སྣང་གི་རང་གཞན་མགོ་གཡོགས་པར་བྱེད་པ་རྣམས་བློ་གཏན་ལ་དབབ་ཅིང་གཟུ་བོར་གནས་པ་གལ་ཆེ་བར་སྣང་ངོ་།

Gomtsül[21] and some of the forefathers of the Practice Lineage.

As for more details, you should carry through with your practice, gain understanding from the inner master that is your own mind and from the outer master that is the teachings and instructions of the realized siddhas. Thus, bring yourself to the level of *exhaustion of concepts and phenomena*.

There are people like me who, without being perfected through the karmic continuity of former training, are satisfied with a couple of years of practicing the Dharma of comfort. When afterwards they pretend to have reached full realization, they fool both themselves and others with superficial benefit. It seems more important to establish true understanding and be honest.

༄ བཞི་པ་སྒོམ་བསྐྱངས་པས་ས་ལམ་བགྲོད་ཚུལ་ནི།

སྤྱིར་མཚན་ཉིད་ཐེག་པ་ནས་བཤད་པའི་ལམ་རིམ་ཅན་དུ་སྦྱངས་པ་སྣང་ཚུལ་ཡོན་ཏན་གྱི་ཁྱད་པར་དུ་བྱས་པ་དང་།

འདིར་སྒོམ་གཞུག་མའི་ལམ་གཅིག་ཆོད་དུ་སྦྱངས་པ་རང་བཞིན་གྱི་ངོ་བོས་ཁྱད་པར་དུ་བྱས་པ་གཉིས་མཐར་ཐུག་ཏུ་འདྲ་ཡང་གནས་སྐབས་སུ་རྣམ་པ་མི་མཐུན་ལ།

འོན་ཀྱང་ས་ཚོད་ལམ་ཚོད་བགྲོད་པའི་ཚུལ་ནི། དང་པོར་བྱིན་རླབས་ཀྱི་ལམ་ལ་ཞུགས་པ་ནས་སྒོམ་རྩེ་གཅིག་གི་ངོ་བོ་མཐོང་ཞིང་རྩལ་རྫོགས་པའི་བར་ལས་དང་པོ་པའི་ས་ཚོགས་ལམ་གྱི་སྐབས་དང་།

སྒོམ་སྤྲོས་བྲལ་གསུམ་གྱི་བར་ནི་མོས་པས་སྤྱོད་པའི་ས་སྦྱོར་ལམ་གྱི་སྐབས་དང་།

སྒོམ་རོ་གཅིག་གསུམ་དང་སྒོམ་མེད་ཆུང་འབྲིང་ནི་ས་དང་པོ་མཐོང་བའི་ལམ་དང་ས་གཉིས་པ་ནས་བཅུ་པའི་བར་གྱི་སྒོམ་ལམ་གྱི་སྐབས་ཅི་རིགས་དང་། སྒོམ་མེད་ཆེན་པོ་ནི་སངས་རྒྱས་ཀྱི་ས་མཐར་ཕྱིན་པའི་ལམ་དང་འགྲོར་རོ།།

འཕྲལ་དུ་གནས་ལུགས་ཀྱི་རང་འགྲོས་སྐྱོངས་པ་ལས་རྒྱུའི་ཐེག་པ་ནས་བཤད་པའི་ལམ་མ་བསྒོམས་ཤིང་།

Part Four

The Way to Traverse the Paths and Bhumis through Meditation Training

Generally speaking, there is the path of gradual training explained in the philosophical vehicles, which specifies manifest qualities, and the present meditation practice, the path of training instantaneously in the original state that ascertains your natural essence. These two are ultimately alike while being temporarily dissimilar. Nevertheless, here is the description of the paths and bhumis and the way in which they are traversed.

From the initial entering upon the path of blessings up to seeing the essence and perfecting the strength of the meditation of One-Pointedness corresponds to the duration of the level of a beginner and the path of accumulation.

Up to and including the three meditation stages of Simplicity corresponds to the duration of the level of devoted conduct and the path of joining.

The three meditation stages of One Taste and the lesser and medium Nonmeditation corresponds to the duration from the level of the first bhumi and the path of seeing, as well as to the path of cultivation from the second to the tenth bhumi.

The greater Nonmeditation corresponds to the level of buddhahood and the path of consummation.

དེ་ལ་བརྟེན་ནས་དེ་ལ་བཤད་པའི་ལམ་རྟགས་ཀྱང་མི་འོང་སྟེ།

སྒོམ་མེད་ཆེན་པོའི་རྩལ་རྫོགས་དུས་སྣང་ཚུལ་གྱི་ཡོན་ཏན་ཐམས་ཅད་ཅིག་ཆར་ལྷུན་གྲུབ་ཏུ་འབྱུང་བར་བཞེད་པ་ཡིན་ལ།

འོན་ཀྱང་གསང་སྔགས་ཐབས་ཀྱི་ལམ་དང་བསྲེས་ནས་བསྒོམས་ན་སྔགས་ཀྱི་ལམ་རྟགས་ཀྱི་རིམ་པ་འཆར་བ་བཤད་དོ།།

སྒོམ་རྣལ་འབྱོར་བཞི་གསུམ་བཅུ་གཉིས་དང་མཚན་ཉིད་ཐེག་པའི་ས་ལམ་ཞིབ་ཆར་སྦྱར་བ་འགའ་རེ་སྣང་ཡང་ཞིབ་ཆར་གྲུངས་འགྲིགས་པ་དཀའ་བ་ཡིན་ནོ།།

དེ་ལྟར་བྱིན་རླབས་ཀྱི་ལམ་ངེས་དོན་ཕྱག་རྒྱ་ཆེན་པོའི་ཁྲིད་ཆེན་འདི་ཕལ་ཆེར་སྦྱོང་ཐོག་ནས་དྲངས་ཤིང་སྦྱོང་བ་མ་ཐོབ་པ་ལ་དག་ཀྱང་སྒྲུབ་བརྒྱུད་གོང་མ་རྣམས་ཀྱི་མན་ངག་ལ་བརྟེན་ནས་རྟོག་གེའི་བཟོ་དང་སྤེལ་སྦྱོར་གྱིས་མ་བཅིངས་པར་གོ་བདེར་བཤད་ཅིང་།

རྒྱབ་རྟེན་གྱི་ལུང་སྦྱོར་ལ་སོགས་པའང་མང་བའི་འཇིགས་པས་འདིར་མ་བྲིས་ལ་རྒྱས་པར་གཞན་དུ་ཤེས་པར་བྱའོ།།

ཉམས་སུ་ལེན་པའི་ཚེ་རང་རང་གི་བློ་ཚོད་དང་བསྟུན་པའི་སྒོམ་ལུགས་གཙོ་བོར་གནས་པ་རང་ལ་དྲིན་ཆེ་བ་ཞིག་བྱ་སྟེ། འདིར་བཤད་པའི་ཚིག་རིས་ཀྱི་གོ་བ་ཁྱེར་ནས་དྲེད་པོ་ཁའི་ལྟ་བ་མཐོན་པོ་ཆོས་རྒྱུས་མཁན་ཉམས་ལེན་ལ་སྦྱོང་བ་མ་ཐོན་པ་གཏན་མི་བྱ་བ་གལ་ཆེའོ།།

Presently, since you simply sustain the way of the natural state and do not practice the path explained in the causal vehicles, the signs of that path will therefore also not appear. However, it is held that all the manifest qualities will appear simultaneously and spontaneously once you have perfected the strength of greater Nonmeditation.

Nevertheless, if you practice by mingling with the Secret Mantra path of means, it is explained that the successive signs of the Mantra path do appear.

There do exist several ways of combining in a detailed way the twelvefold meditation training of the three-times-four yogas with the paths and bhumis of the philosophical vehicles, but it is complicated to organize them meticulously.

Thus, this major guidance text for the blessed Mahamudra path of definitive meaning should customarily be taught through personal experience. For those who have not gained such experience, I have made use of the pithy instructions of the forefathers of the Practice Lineage to explain this in a way that is simple to understand, without convoluting it with scholarly verbiage and structures. Afraid of overloading it with supportive quotations, I have refrained from doing so. You can find such details elsewhere.[22]

When it comes to bringing this into your personal experience, be kind to yourself by honestly applying a method of meditating that suits your individual capacity. By all means, it is essential to desist from taking what you understand of these words and insensitively spout high

འདིར་སྨྲས་པ།

གྲུབ་པའི་སྐྱེས་མཆོག་རྣམས་ཀྱི་རྡོ་རྗེའི་གསུང་།

སྙིགས་དུས་བྱིས་པའི་བློ་ལ་འཕྲུགས་པར་གྱུར།

ཕྱོགས་ཙམ་གསལ་བའི་ཁྲིད་གཞུང་ཉུང་ཟབ་རྣམས།

སྨྱོང་བ་སྐྱེས་ཚེ་འདི་བྱའི་ཞུགས་ཐབས་བྲལ།

ཐོས་སྟོབས་སྦྱོན་སྦྱངས་ལྡན་པ་མ་རྟོགས་པས།

མན་ངག་འཐོར་བ་བསྒྲིག་པར་ཤེས་པ་ཉུང་།

དེ་ཕྱིར་ལམ་རིམ་གསལ་བའི་ཁྲིད་གཞུང་འདི།

རྣལ་འབྱོར་བདག་གི་བླ་མེད་མཆོད་སྦྱིན་ཡིན།

སྒྲུབ་བརྒྱུད་འཛིན་པའི་རྩ་བརྒྱུད་བླ་མ་ལ།

བྱིན་རླབས་རྟོགས་པ་སྩོལ་བའི་མཎྜལ་མཛོད།

རྟོགས་པ་མངོན་དུ་གྱུར་པའི་སྒོམ་ཆེན་ལ།

གསལ་འདེབས་ཡིད་ཆེས་བསྐྱེད་པའི་མཆོད་པ་མཛོད།

ཉམས་རྟོགས་སྨྱུ་གུ་རྒྱས་པའི་སྒོམ་ཆུང་ལ།

ཐེ་ཚོམ་གཅོད་པའི་ངེས་ཤེས་དགའ་སྟོན་མཛོད།

views. Please avoid becoming a "Dharma expert" with no practical experience!

Concluding Verses

The vajra speech of sublime accomplished masters
Is distorted in the minds of the childish people
of the dark age.
The few profound guidance texts that clarify some parts
Give no final support to how or when experiences arise.

Apart from those who possess the strength of learning
and former training,
Only a few people can assemble the fragments
of oral advice.
My guidance text to clarify the stages of the path
Is therefore the unexcelled offering from this yogi.

For the root and lineage masters who uphold
the Practice Lineage,
May it be a mandala that bestows blessings
and realization!
For advanced meditators who have brought forth
realization,
May it be an offering that reminds and inspires trust.

For seasoned meditators who nurture the seedlings
of experience and realization,
May it be a banquet of certainty that cuts through doubt.

སྒྲོང་ཞེན་ཅན་གྱི་བསྟོན་ལྡན་སྒོམ་ཕྲུག་ལ།

ལྟ་ལོག་སྒོམ་སྐྱོན་སེལ་བའི་སྦྱིན་གཏོང་མཛོད།

སྒྲོང་བྲལ་ཐོས་ལོ་བསགས་པའི་བྱ་བྲལ་ལ།

གནས་ལུགས་ཡོན་ཏན་ཐོབ་པའི་ཕ་འབབས་མཛོད།

མ་རྟོགས་ལོག་ལྟའི་སྐྱོན་གྱི་ཉེས་ཚོགས་རྣམས།

དམ་པ་རྣམས་ལ་ཀུན་ཏུ་བཤགས་པར་བགྱི།

འདི་ཡི་དགེ་བས་བདག་དང་འགྲོ་བ་ཀུན།

ཕྱག་ཆེན་རྟོགས་པ་མྱུར་ཏུ་མཐར་ཕྱིན་ཤོག།

ཅེས་པ་ཡང་སློབ་བུ་སྒོམ་ཆེན་འགའ་ཞིག་གིས་ཕྱག་ཆེན་ཁྲིད་ཡིག་ཕུགས་ཐེབས་ཆེ་བ་ཞིག་བྱས་ན་ཞེས་བསྐུལ་བ་ལ་བརྟེན་ནས་སྨྲ་བོ་པ་མཉྫ་ལའི་མིང་ཅན་གྱིས་ལུག་ལོ་ཟླ་བ་བཞི་པའི་དཀར་ཕྱོགས་ལ་གདན་ས་ཆེན་པོ་དཔལ་དྭགས་ལ་སྒོམ་པོའི་སྒྲུབ་སྡེར་སྦྱར་བའི་ཡི་གེ་པ་ནི་བཀྲ་ཤིས་དོན་གྲུབ་ཅེས་བྱ་བས་བགྱིས་པ་སྟེ།

འདིས་ཀྱང་འགྲོ་བ་མཐའ་དག་ལ་དགེ་ལེགས་སུ་གྱུར་ཅིག།

སརྦ་ད་མངྒ་ལམ།

དགེའོ།།

For apprentice meditators, diligent but clinging
to experiences,
May it be a bounty that dispels wrong views
and faulty meditation.

For idle Dharma people who only gather data
without experience,
May it be the legacy for attaining the natural state's
qualities.
For all the shortcomings of my ignorance and
misunderstanding
I apologize forever to all sublime beings.

Through this virtue may all beings
Swiftly perfect the realization of Mahamudra.

Colophon

This text is based on requests from several of my meditator disciples to write a decisive and reliable guidance manual on Mahamudra. The one from Gampo with the name Mangala (Tashi) composed it during the waxing part of the fourth lunar month in the Year of the Sheep at the retreat center of the great seat, the glorious Dakla Gampo, with the help of the scribe Tashi Döndrub. May it bring virtuous goodness to all beings. Sarvada mangalam. May it be virtuous!

Translator's Colophon

It has been a profound privilege and joy to fulfill Khenchen Thrangu Rinpoche's wish that an English version of this text be made available. With his oral teachings at two Namo Buddha Seminars and his additional clarifications as guidance, this first attempt was made by Erik Pema Kunsang and Michael Tweed at Nagi Gompa hermitage, April 2001.

It was Rinpoche's wish to include the Tibetan script to facilitate further teaching and understanding. His student Christopher B. Barstow did the typing. Thanks to Khenpo Jigmey and Khenpo Pema Gyaltsen for proofreading the Tibetan, and also to my wife Marcia for checking the manuscript. Special credit is owed to Larry Mermelstein of the Nalanda Translation Committee for his extensive review and suggestions. The endnotes, as well as imperfections and faults, are mine.

May this bring countless beings in contact with their original nature.

Endnotes

[1] The gradual stages of the path for the three types of individuals are embodied in the *Jewel Ornament of Liberation*. It is therefore advisable to have studied those teachings prior to this book.

[2] Tuck your chin in slightly.

[3] Wind *(rlung)* here refers to imbalances of energy currents in the body.

[4] The Tibetan word for 'aware' here is *gsal ba*. It is often translated as luminous, cognizant, clear, lucid, wakeful, etc.

[5] In the following text, this principle of 'not being a definable entity' is also referred to as intangible, indescribable, not pinpointing or unidentifiable.

[6] Thrangu Rinpoche mentioned here that it is sometimes necessary that the instructor says the opposite of the truth to see if the student will 'take the bait'. This will expose intellectual understanding.

[7] Thrangu Rinpoche mentioned that meditation famine means a weak and unsteady type of practice with no foundation for progress.

[8] The word for 'meditating' (*sgom skyong ba*) can also be translated as *maintaining the practice* or *continuing the training*.

[9] Phrased differently: "your meditation practice is simple and easy to maintain."

[10] Involvement in practices for gathering the accumulation of merit and purifying the obscuration of negative karma rather than training in Mahamudra is also known as *losing the view in the conduct*.

[11] In this context, *essence* is a synonym for the natural state.

[12] Thrangu Rinpoche mentioned that the four yogas in this context are to be practiced with recognition of the nature of mind.

[13] Not pinpointing means to remain open, not identifying, labeling or fixating.

[14] Literally, "This is not working! Something else is needed!"

[15] *Revealing the Hidden* is entitled *Gabpa Ngönjung.*

[16] The ***kusulu*** offering and giving refers to the Chö practice.

[17] Imagine being struck by an even more horrible disease.

[18] This is why Simplicity literally means *absence of constructs*.

[19] Among 'inducing circumstances' are compassion, devotion, perseverance and intelligence.

[20] 'Dualistic' is inserted in front of consciousness (*rnam shes*) so as to distinguish it from original wakefulness (*ye shes*).

[21] Lord Gomtsül (*rje sgom tshul*) is the nephew of Gampopa, also known as Tsültrim Nyingpo (*tshul khrims snying po*).

[22] Quotations from masters of the Practice Lineage are found in *Moonbeams of Mahamudra*, (*Mahamudra*), Shambhala Publications, 1986.